Martin

GW01464479

THE MEDIA
and how to use it

VERITAS

First published 1988 by
Veritas Publications
7-8 Lower Abbey Street
Dublin 1

Copyright © Martin Tierney 1988

ISBN 1 85390 011 7

Acknowledgements
The author and publishers are grateful to the following for permission to reproduce extracts from their copyright material: The World Association for Christian Communication, *Media Development*, 1/1984 and *Journal of the World Association for Christian Communication*, Vol XX, 1983; Sonolux, extract by Ruedi Hofmann, from *Group Media Journal*; Lion Publishing, *Silicon Society*, David Lyon; McCrimmon Publishing Co. Ltd, *Buying Time*, Peter Elvy, quoting Paul Crouch; The Press Council, London, *Guidance on Procedure for Complainants*; Twenty-Third Publications, *Memoirs and Memories*, Gary McEoin; Routledge & Kegan Paul Ltd in association with the International Institute of Communications, *Broadcasting in Ireland*, Desmond Fisher; OCIC, extract from *OCC — Info* 1983/3; Comedia Publishing, *fourth Rate Estate*, Tom Baistow; Sage Publications, *The Myth of Information Technology*, Michael Traber (ed); Leuven University Press/Uitgeverij Peeters, Leuven 1983, *The 1980 Synod of Bishops: On The Role of the Family*, J. Grootaers and J. Selling; National Union of Journalists, London, *NUJ Code of Professional Conduct*; Heinemann Publishers International Ltd, *Editing and Design*, Harold Evans; Sir Robin Day, *Television: A Personal Report* (published 1961 by Hutchinson).

Cover design by Angela Young
Typesetting by Printset & Design Ltd, Dublin
Printed in the Republic of Ireland by The Leinster Leader Ltd

Contents

Part One

Media Developments and Gospel Values

Introduction

The media is both hated and courted, sometimes by the same people at different times! The British poet Auden wrote that the media is 'intended to be consumed like food, forgotten and replaced by a new dish'. On the other hand, a television star of the 1950s, Bishop Fulton Sheen, said 'spiritually, radio and TV are beautiful examples of the inspired wisdom of the ages'. You take your pick! Whatever side you are on, the mass media is here to stay. Ignoring it, as some pretend to do, will not make it go away.

Ever since Paul of Tarsus took his ink and reed or sharpened goose quill and scraped his epistles on papyrus of inferior quality, the Christian Church has tried to communicate the message of salvation. The Church has attempted to use the best means available at any given time. We are in an electronic age and new demands will be made on those committed to the proclamation of the gospel to explore and harness the new media.

Specialisation has become an addiction. The pursuit of doctorates and master's degrees and diplomas pushes the generalist to the periphery of the action. Specialists weave an aura of mystery around their area of competence that intimidates the generalist. Media is too pervasive to be left to the specialist. Today's newspaper wraps tomorrow's fish and chips, but it's read and handled by the proverbial person in-the-street. Sophisticated media reach from the broad Punjab beneath the foothills of the Himalayas to the Mexican Plaza of Santo Domingo, where today *evangelistas*, letter writers with obsolete typewriters, perform for a few pennies a service of love. Professionalism is important. So is training. However, the generalist can use the means of communication most readily consumed, understood, and accessible to the people. The Church cannot allow herself to arrive once more 'breathless and late'.

One piece of humbug propagated by media personnel is the notion that 'the public have a right to know'. The implication of this is that the media have a right, perhaps even a duty, to reveal! The right to know theory was put to the test during the American invasion of Grenada and Britain's sortie into the Falklands. In the former case, the media was completely excluded initially; in the latter, it was severely muzzled. Were the public up in arms? Public analyst, William Schneider, writing in the *National Journal* claimed that: 'Judging from the evidence, the public did not feel particularly deprived. The polls showed considerable approval of the decision to keep the press out. Indeed, resentment of the press seemed to explode in the aftermath of Grenada.' (*The National Journal*, 4 February 1984) A *Los Angeles Times* survey confirmed Schneider's view.

In 1982 a national opinion poll conducted by the National Opinion Research Center in the United States recorded that only a paltry 13.7% of the public claimed to have 'a great deal of confidence in the press'. Even banks enjoyed more public confidence, with a 24.1% rating. A similar poll conducted six years earlier in 1976 gave the media a 29% rating.

Unease about the media is not confined to America. The Press Council in Britain lashed out against the 'ferocious and callous harassment' of relatives and friends by the press in the Peter Sutcliffe or so-called 'Yorkshire Ripper' case.

In the Irish Report of the European Value System study, the media came second last, just ahead of the trades unions, in a list of ten national institutions in which the Irish people had confidence. In fact, while 53% of those surveyed claimed to have a great deal of confidence in the Church, only a meagre 10% said the same of the press (*Irish Values and Attitudes*, Dominican Publications, 1984, p. 177).

Fear appears to be the predominant reaction to the media. Lord Reith, the 'father' of the BBC, admitted of television that he 'was frightened of it from the start'. Even the late President Eamonn de Valera articulated a fear when he inaugurated Ireland's first television service in 1961.

He said: 'I must admit that sometimes when I think of television and radio and their immense power, I feel somewhat afraid. Like atomic energy it can be used for incalculable good but it can also do irreparable harm.'

Unease with the media does not come just from the Church. Ron Todd, General Secretary of the powerful Transport and

General Workers Union in Britain, delivered a swingeing attack on the 'outrageously biased and partisan' tabloid press. He said: 'Over the past decade there has been a measurable and dramatic decline in the standards of the popular press. I believe that the standards of the popular press have become so corrupt as to create a cultural imbalance, which is a threat to the health of democracy itself' ('Media — the future of democracy' — a lecture delivered at the London School of Economics, May 1987).

Even those associated with the media are beginning to recognise, albeit a little late, that the credibility of the media is at a very low ebb. Geoffrey Goodman, a former assistant editor of the *Daily Mirror*, writing in the periodical *The Tablet*, claimed that 'lies are no longer the prerogative of government "news management" — they are now freely, and almost unblushingly, produced within the word trade itself. And, like so many other forms of virus, they feed on themselves.' The electronic media did not escape the pen of Mr Goodman: 'The decline in the quality of newspaper journalism has its matching reaction in the electronic media, especially in television. Numerous television producers in the BBC and independent networks have complained, in private, about the "ratings" pressures on them to jazz up their programmes.' (*The Tablet*, June 1987)

The print media hit a new low when the *Chicago Sun Times*, frustrated in its attempts to 'expose' corruption in city government, purchased a dilapidated bar in the seamy northside of the city and, using reporters disguised as bartenders, managed to entrap municipal officials. Then there was the case of Janet Cooke of the *Washington Post* who landed a Pulitzer Prize for a fabricated story about an eight-year-old heroin addict called Jimmy. Jimmy was a composite, a fiction, located so compellingly on the streets of Washington that the hoax fooled the editors of the *Post* and the Pulitzer Board.

The relatively new phenomenon of 'cheque-book journalism', as in the case of Peter Sutcliffe, the so-called Yorkshire Ripper, who was convicted of killing at least thirteen women, most of them prostitutes, drew criticism from the Press Council, in Britain. The Council's report described reporters as offering 'blood money' for any exclusive background revelations.

11

The Media and How to Use It embodies much of my own personal experience. I have also picked the brains of media experts in Ireland and elsewhere. The reader will quickly realise that this is a book written by a very general practitioner, offered as an aid rather than a solution, for those who have or will have occasion to deal with the media.

However, it is not enough to learn off a few handy rules of thumb on how to handle a radio or television interview or how to write a press release. I believe that if this book is to be of any real benefit, the material has to be placed in the context of developments in mass media over the past decade. Some questions spring to mind immediately — How does the media work? What makes news? What are the implications of the communications revolution raging all around us? Does the Roman Catholic Church have a view on the mass media? If so, what is it? I have expanded my original intention to encompass these and other additional questions.

While researching the material for this work I became conscious that concentrated interest in the media is the preserve of the academic. I found it difficult to obtain popular and general reading on media matters. This fact encouraged me to persevere on the many occasions when I felt like running up the white flag.

I have written this book in popular language to help the general practitioner to gain some knowledge of the extraordinary developments in the means of communication over the past generation. I have tried to situate my message within a pastoral context, always keeping in mind the priest, sister, brother or layperson who is anxious to refine the proclamation of the gospel message to the best means available.

In the second section of the book I have attempted to be simple and practical. Getting in touch with and using the media of print, radio and television must increasingly occupy the minds of those who are serious about reaching the people of today with the gospel. I have been a media addict for years. As a youngster I raced down the road to greet my father on his return from work and tried to be the first in the house to read the latest instalment of Mandrake the Magician in the now defunct *Evening Mail*. I have had the opportunity of watching the experts at work. Some of the lessons I have learned through practical experience. I am grateful for the help I have received, and I would like, in particular, to acknowledge the encouragement of Fr Myles O'Brien Reilly, Director of Communications for the Archdiocese of San Francisco, who generously allowed me to draw from much of his published work. Des Cryan of the Catholic Press and Information Office in Dublin read the first draft of the typescript and encourged me to continue. I am grateful to the late Archbishop Dermot Ryan who had enough confidence in me to asign me to pursue an apostolate in communications. I would like to thank the dedicated staff of Veritas.

Just before we went to print my brother-in-law, John Byrne, went to his eternal reward. I would like to dedicate this book to his memory.

Those who work in the media have a difficult job. They have to produce exciting copy, meet deadlines, traipse to uninteresting locations, criticise even their friends, be disliked by many people and, they provide an invaluable service to the whole community. I would like to thank them all for the work they do on our behalf.

My hope is that *The Media and How to Use It* will inform and help those interested in media matters and will assist others likely to be called upon to be spokespersons at the wrong end of the microphone or camera.

Chapter One

A Media for Good or Evil?

The car radio makes even the worst traffic jam tolerable. Surrounded by frustrated motorists I listened intently to a priest being interviewed by a superbly professional journalist. As the aptly chosen and slightly barbed questions flowed, my clerical friend became more deeply enmeshed in the web of his own confusion. He couldn't extricate himself. He was made to appear bumbling, reactionary and incompetent. I am not blaming the interviewer. She had done her homework! Neither am I blaming the priest, he did his best, but he was obviously ill-prepared to face a professional interviewer. It was a no contest situation!

Reflecting on this experience, I continue to be amazed at the cavalier fashion with which many people treat the media. While media personnel brief themselves, avail of researchers and determine their line of questioning in advance, the interviewee appears in the 'Emperor's new clothes' and suffers the consequences!

As media personnel become even more professional, the public, many possible media targets among them, become less willing to be trained and briefed in an area which has been honed to a fine art. This is particularly true of Church personnel. Lack of expertise on the part of the interviewee means that a 'hidden agenda', so often part of the mass media's strategy, goes unrecognised.

Returning to my clerical interviewee mentioned above, I thought 'Would a handbook giving simple hints for dealing with the media be of assistance?' The result is this book — a volume slightly larger than I had originally intended.

Ever since 'Deep Throat' passed into the English language as the pseudonym of a confidential journalistic source, media credibility has roller-coasted downwards. Woodward and Bernstein, through painstaking investigative journalism, gave The *Washington Post* — and by association the mass media generally — unprecedented respectability. When the world's most powerful establishment figure of the time, Richard Nixon, was toppled, 'open season' was declared by the media on all establishments and institutions, with the exception of the media itself. The year 1972 marked the nadir of media excellence.

In this chapter I would like to give a brief overview of both the negative and positive aspects of the mass media. This book is not intended as an exercise in 'media bashing', so I would encourage you, the reader, whatever your prejudices, to persevere.

Information is increasingly viewed as a commodity to be packaged and marketed for profit. It often masquerades in self-righteous fashion as a surrogate for you, the people — lifting stones, peering down manholes, scavenging on tipheads — to bring you the news. Conflict and scandal are caviar to the media. But now the fight back is on. The media as surrogate is a notion that is being challenged with increasing frequency. It is generally recognised that the bottom line for the mass media is, What will sell the paper or deliver the advertisers? Obviously this is an exaggeration, but there is sufficient truth in the accusation to cause growing concern about the methods and the content of the mass media in the developed world. Journalists are seldom motivated by the high-principled desire to protect the public. Lyndon Johnson once claimed that: 'Reporters are puppets. They simply respond to the pull of the most powerful strings!' Like many of those in other walks of life, personal advancement, increased circulation and just plain making a living, are to the forefront of their minds. There are isolated but notable exceptions like John Pilger, Robert Fisk and the late James Cameron.

The latest example of scandal journalism involved the former deputy chairman of Britain's Conservative Party, Jeffrey Archer.

He was entrapped by *News of the World* journalists who accused him of consorting with a prostitute. Then the tabloid *Star* newspaper compounded the original libel by repeating it, in uglier detail, five days later. They reckoned without Archer's brave decision to take the newspapers to court and win a victory settlement of £500,000 in damages!

Current practice seems to demand of journalists that they produce confrontational copy. Whether it is a television or radio programme or a current affairs item in a daily newspaper it is becoming increasingly evident that 'the person-in-the-street' has little to offer apart from an occasional 'vox-pop' to add a little colour. There appears to be a growing compulsion to present only the views of those representing the extreme spectra of an argument. The middle ground is invariably lost. It has become almost axiomatic that television is confrontational. Put opposing forces together, let them loose and enjoy the ensuing cockfight. Feathers fly and blood is spilt. It may increase the blood lust of the viewer — but does it add to the sum of human wisdom?

Note the vocabulary of the media — slam; lash; ban; flay; hit-out; slash; reject; crisis. These words almost invariably appear in our daily headlines. Now read the story! The connection between the headlines and the story is often tenuous, to say the least. This constant parade of a hackneyed pugilistic vocabulary can even fan the flames of controversy. It is interesting that the media is increasingly being castigated for being unhelpful — by *both* sides in industrial disputes.

More and more, the yellow press garnish their newspapers with self-righteous exposés of scandals in high places and, at the same time, titillate their readers with pictures of naked women.

There was a view current, and correctly so, that the media held a mirror up to life and reflected that image for its readers, listeners or viewers. It was the objective observer of life, the 'fly-on-the-wall'. Fact and comment were easily distinguishable. The new crusading and partisan media no longer accepts that view. The media aims to help the public to change their minds. But can it? At the height of Ireland's referendum to insert an anti-abortion clause in the Constitution, in one typical week the column inches devoted to the anti-amendment position were double the amount given over to the pro-amendment argument. (cf. *Fair and Accurate? — the Amendment and the Press —* Timothy O'Sullivan, Veritas Publications, 1984). Yet the final result of the referendum showed overwhelming support for inserting the anti-abortion clause into the Constitution. So much for the mirror-up-to-life theory of media practice! A partisan media can distort a national debate but it doesn't yet seem to have sufficient influence to convince readers and listeners to change their viewpoints!

It is becoming increasingly difficult to assess the objectivity of the media due to the widespread use of unidentified sources to build up stories. What value has the statement 'A government source claimed. . . .'? Was it a minister, an office cleaner, a junior executive officer or a party hack? What weight is the reader meant to give to such a source? Take comments like 'critics claim' or 'an increasing number of priests feel incensed' — how many critics? Is the increase from two priests to three? In fairness, attempts to manipulate the media by frequent off-the-record briefing, beloved of politicians and others, contributes significantly to media ambivalence. The media consumer must be finding it even more difficult to determine the accuracy of media statements.

There is no accurate way of establishing where media personnel in Ireland stand on social, political or religious issues. However, in a shrinking world, I wonder is Ireland any different from America? An American survey (published in *Public Opinion —* a journal of the American Enterprise Institute for Public Policy Research, in November 1981) revealed that the outlook of the media elite is secular. Only 50% subscribe to any religion and only 8% said they were regular churchgoers; 90% agreed that a woman has a right to decide for herself whether to have an abortion; 54% said they did not regard adultery as wrong, and only 15% saw extra-marital affairs as being wrong. It is only the lone journalistic voice that will flow against the current of the secular liberal stance adopted by most media personnel.

So much for the negative aspects of our mass media. There

is a reverse side to the coin. A free and unfettered media can be the arteries through which the oxygen of truth reaches the public. Garnished truth perhaps, at times even embellished and exaggerated truth — but truth nevertheless, and enough of it to ensure the continuing existence of a healthy democracy. Why is it that the fiercest struggles between revolutionary factions are for the channels of information? Any coup d'état depends for its success on seizing the radio and television stations and muzzling the newspapers quickly and efficiently. The suppression of a free press is a sign that all is not well in the state of Denmark! Perhaps one of the worst moves on the part of President Daniel Ortega of Nicaragua was the supression of the fiercely independent newspaper, *La Pensa*. Even loyal supporters of the regime thought they smelled a rat! On the other hand, it is generally acknowledged that **Radio Veritas** of the Philippines played a significant part in the final overthrow of the corrupt Marcos regime.

A free press exposes corruption and continually subjects the power brokers in society to critical scrutiny. Would Haldeman, Erlichman, Mitchell and Nixon ever have been brought to account if America hadn't a free press? It was the film **Missing** that finally convinced the world of the duplicity of American foreign policy in Chile. A made-for-television film, **The Day After**, provoked worldwide debate on the threat of nuclear war. **Full Metal Jacket** exposed the horrors and futility of the Vietnam escapade. The media can reveal the cockroaches!

One man who has learned to use the media with skill is the Archbishop of Capetown, Desmond Tutu. A few days after his enthronement, he wrote: 'The world Church was there. What South Africa could become — what it will become — unfolded before our eyes.' The world was there through the eyes of the international media. Through relentless pursuit by the international media, the gross injustices of the apartheid system have been exposed, to such an extent that the government finally muzzled the media.

A clever campaign orchestrated by Richard Rodgers brought the plight of Russian poet Irina Ratushinskaya to notice. Rodgers, an Anglican clergyman, lived in a cage in the crypt of a

Birmingham church for the forty days of Lent, reproducing as far as possible the circumstances of Irina's imprisonment. Irina was eventually released.

'Daddy, I love you very much', were the last words of Enniskillen nurse Marie Wilson. She spoke, huddled beside her father, under the debris of a vicious IRA bombing. However, it was the moving radio and television interview granted later by her father that moved a nation. He said, 'My wife and I don't bear any grudges. We don't feel any ill-will towards those who were responsible for this. We see it as God's plan even though we might not understand it. I shall pray for those people tonight and every night.' His interview demonstrated the media's powerful potential for good.

Famine and injustice have often been exposed through the courageous efforts of media personnel. I was fortunate enough to accompany a group of Irish journalists to Ethiopia at the height of the 1985 famine. I was impressed by their diligence and the accuracy of their reports. It was Michael Buerk of the BBC who first stumbled upon this horrific famine and, through his initial reports, alerted the world to the suffering that was imminent.

Sport is one of the areas of life that has benefited most by media exposure. Golfing buffs watched late into the night and early morning during the Ryder Cup jostle with America. The Americas Cup has brought the sport of sailing from being the preserve of the few into the living rooms of the world. Soccer has benefited from a televised World Cup, and the craze of jogging probably owes much to the massive reporting of the Olympic Games. Even snooker, formerly a feature of a 'misspent' youth, has become a popular mass appeal sport. Televised snooker commands an audience of millions.

The possibility of gaining a university degree is open even to the sick, housebound and imprisoned, through the medium of television. Schools television and children's programming contributes significantly to the educational possibilities of a mass audience.

An encouraging sign is that the fight back against a biased and slovenly media is in some cases being spearheaded by the media itself. The Channel Four programme, **Right to Reply**, presents the viewers with the opportunity to subject the programmers to interrogation and forces them to defend themselves against allegations of unfairness or bias. The **Video Box**, situated strategically around Britain, ensures that the 'right to reply' can be availed of by a large number of people. In addition, Channel Four also affords viewers the opportunity to present their points of view on the daily **Comment** slot. The BBC now offers a monthly exchange between viewers and television makers in its **Network** programme.

In a quite unique article, *Sunday Times* columnist, Carol Sarler, admitted exploiting the emotional vulnerability and need of friendship of an Edinburgh prostitute with AIDS, in order to obtain a good colour story for the paper. She 'befriended' Karen, so much so that she fell 'hook, line and sinker for me and my act as bestest friend'. Sarler said of journalists that 'we are at our most dangerous when we use feelings, subtlety and decency ...when we prey not so much on fear of exposure as on loneliness and the need of so many people for anyone who feels like a friend'. (*The Sunday Times*, 13 September 1987). This published admission may be the first swallow in the media's own attempt to respond to the odium in which it is held by large sections of the public.

Any newspaper worth its salt will reserve space in a 'Letters to the Editor' column for the readers' viewpoint. Some of the quality papers are generous in allowing readers the opportunity to contradict or correct their own journalists.

In fairness, it must be said that the public is never fully aware of the constraints of time and space imposed on the media. The tyranny of the deadline or the confines of the fifty-minute documentary inevitably means that much will be left unsaid or some facts will fail to be confirmed.

Philip Graham, one of America's most celebrated publishers, described the press as 'the first rough draft of history'. The historians of the future will rely in some measure on the newspapers of the present to recount the wars and famines and mores of today. Reporters garner the immediacy of an event that literature will never capture. The conflict in Northern Ireland is written in graphic raw detail by today's journalists. That's where future historians will find unparalleled resource material. Have a look in the drawers at home! It is the odd home that hasn't collected the newspaper cuttings on family successes and achievements. We all want our place in history and so our birth and death notices become family heirlooms.

Chapter Two

The Communications Explosion

I can recall with ease my grandmother lighting the oil lamp in the old family homestead as evening gathered. Its light was strong and sufficient to reach into the corners of the flagged kitchen with its open hearth. Butter was churned and made completely by hand. Milk went to the creamery by donkey and cart. Ploughing depended on rather primitive implements and a sturdy horse that grazed in the nearby haggart. The food was nourishing and simple. Bacon from the pig killed yearly, together with large floury potatoes, cabbage from the garden and milk were the staples. On special occasions a goose was killed for the table. This was especially true on the feast of St Austin, the patron of the parish, and at Christmas time.

The news was local. Who got what for the beast sold that week in the nearby fair. The weather prospects for saving the hay or footing the turf always generated interested conversation. Returned emigrants, always called 'Yanks' if they came from America, were discussed. Local sports, shooting and fishing and the new curate might also lead to heated conversation. The older people recalled with nostalgia the 'house dance' and the regular card games that filled the fallow hours of wintertime. The connection or 'network' between people was conversation. The unhurried nature of life made space for people to talk and relate.

If there was news percolating in from beyond the parish boundary, it came through the local newspaper, the *Clare Champion*. I cannot recall a national newspaper coming to the house nor have I any recollection of a radio or 'wireless' as it was called in those days. In less than fifty years, a way of life has disappeared. My grandmother, who died in the early sixties, would view today's world as if she were a visitor from another planet.

The inhabitants of a similar cottage today would most likely travel to Dublin regularly. Some would take their holidays in Majorca or the Canary Islands, perhaps even America. A transistor would constantly pour forth music, news, debates on national issues and recordings of the proceedings in the national parliament. At night the television, carrying six or eight channels, would entertain the family with programmes imported from strange and alien cultures. Conversation, formerly the hub of family life, is reduced in quantity and importance. Computers would be handled like the lead pencils of old. Sex, a taboo subject in the past, might be discussed at table. The horse and donkey would no longer graze in the haggart. An antiseptic milking parlour, with electric milking machines, has replaced the byre and one or two cars are parked in the driveway. Transport and communications have become easy. The good old days have gone forever. What have been the effects of the communications and technological explosion of the past forty years?

THE RADIO

In September 1947, I can recall my youthful amazement at being able to listen, from the comforts of my own home in Ireland, to an All Ireland football final between Cavan and Kerry, being played for the first and only time in the Polo Grounds, New York, before a crowd of 35,000. Imagine the Atlantic Ocean being spanned by sound waves!

Over thirty years ago, I hid under the blankets at boarding school to listen, undetected, to the crackling sound of a tiny crystal radio set. I was utterly fascinated by the barely audible voice of a sports commentator, transmitting from a studio all of twenty miles away. My unscientific mind couldn't unravel the mystery of it all.

Then, one Christmas, my father bought a 'radiogram', an enormous piece of furniture. Plastic records replaced the old 78s that we had listened to with contentment on an ancient and battered wind-up gramophone. Now we had a radio that could receive voices and music from foreign stations with clarity. Mass media had truly arrived in the Tierney household. However, radio existed as a mass medium long before it captured my youthful enthusiasm.

It is not generally known that the world's first radio broadcast was made from Dublin, Ireland, on the occasion of the Easter rebellion of April 1916, a rebellion that culminated five years later in the foundation of the Irish Free State. According to Desmond Fisher in *Broadcasting in Ireland*, 'the leaders of the Rising, realising that the British authorities would suppress or destroy the news of it despatched by normal channels, decided to send out the information themselves. They occupied the Irish School of Wireless Telegraphy, across the street from their headquarters at the General Post Office, and repaired a damaged 1.5 kilowatt ship's transmitter which they found there. From 5.30 p.m. that day until noon the next day, when the building had to be abandoned, they sent out signals in Morse code relaying communiqués issued by the leaders of the Rising' (*Broadcasting in Ireland*, Routledge & Kegan Paul, 1978). In 1921, the same year that Ireland achieved independence, the fledgeling British Broadcasting Corporation began its first daily news bulletins.

The potential of radio was not recognised at its discovery. It was, like so many other inventions of the twentieth century, highjacked by the military as a substitute for the telephone. It had one disadvantage — anyone could eavesdrop! It was Lord Northcliffe who first recognised the commercial possibilities and he arranged a promotion stunt for the *Daily Mail*. Dame Nellie Melba, the famous opera singer, was to be broadcast singing from Chelmsford. This event began with a 'long silvery thrill' and ended with 'God Save the King'. It attracted a much larger audience than expected, and so, for the first time, the wireless manufacturers were aware of a potentially huge market.

Then there was the transistor — the scourge of every beach and public park, some would say! Nevertheless, it makes entertainment, news, sport and current events available to a truly international audience. This was brought home to me near the northern Nigerian town of Minna where I saw a youth, without a stitch of clothes on him, herding cattle. In one hand he had a staff, and in the other a blaring two-speaker transistor radio! The cultural implications of mass media transcending national and international boundaries is something that has been given far too little attention by churches or governments.

The problem about radio is that the flow of noise is all one way. You can't talk back! In many countries this is being circumvented through local community radio. For instance, the Swedish broadcasting system has developed local public radio in each of the country's twenty-four provinces. The aim is to allow local groups such as trades unions, political parties, religious organisations, sports clubs, art and culture groups, consumer and tenant associations, environmentalists, ethnic and language groups, to apply for permission to transmit material they have produced in their own or borrowed studios. So far, several hundred local associations and local units of national organisations are participating.

The French too took up the cudgels against the monopoly of their national broadcasting system. A whole range of free or pirate radio stations operate in France. Some of them serve as a neighbourhood medium, providing local news and phone-ins on topical issues. Others are set up to serve current needs; for example workers may form their own station on the occasion of a strike. A third type of station serves political or social activists — ecologists, feminists, homosexuals.

In Italy there are 180-200 stations broadly associated with the Church, vocational and social groups. Again, the rise of the 'free' local radio station was a protest against the monopoly of RAI (Radio Audizioni Italia), the national network.

In the United States, community radio was developed as an alternative to commercial radio. In the 1960s, community radio had a rapid growth among counter-cultural groups which tended to be the more affluent university and intellectual groups. In 1975, a National Federation of Community Broadcasters was established in Washington, which now has about sixty member stations.

It is estimated that the Church owns some 300 radio stations and ten television stations in Latin America.

The rise of the electronic Church in America continues to colour the attitude to broadcasting of the mainline Christian denominations. As early as 1920, listeners to Omaha evangelist R.R. Brown's **Radio Chapel Service** were invited to join the World Radio Congregation, which issued official membership cards.

In England, the Roman Catholics' response to their government's Green Paper, *Radio: Choices and Opportunities*, demonstrates a fear that the airwaves on this side of the Atlantic might easily be taken over by the electronic preachers or even by Islamic fundamentalists. A statement released by the Roman Catholic Bishops of England and Wales makes three recommendations:

a) Religious ownership of a radio station should be forbidden.
b) Existing restrictions on the use of the airwaves to proselytise should be maintained.
c) Religious groups should be subject to the same restrictions as political groups in the matters of advertising and soliciting of money.

The bishops claimed that if religious ownership of a radio station was permissible it would be virtually impossible in certain cases to draw a workable distinction between religious and political opinions. It stated that 'many religious groups have definite and clear political opinions which they promote on religious grounds'.

TELEVISION

On 27 June 1923, the London *Times* carried the following advertisement: 'Seeing by wireless. Inventor of apparatus wishes to hear from someone who will assist (not financially) in making working model. Write Box S 686'. The man lurking behind the box number was John Logie Baird. Just ten years later, the British Broadcasting Corporation, in collaboration with Baird and E.M.I. Marconi launched what was claimed to be the first regular 'high definition' television in the world.

My first view of television was in the late 1950s. The weak, hazy reception from a rooftop aerial mesmerised me. It was an afternoon programme on flower arranging. It didn't matter that the picture was in black and white, nor was I overly concerned by the wobbling screen. The fact that the picture had somehow crossed the Irish Sea, all the way from the BBC studios in London, made the phenomenon truly remarkable.

Today, the television has become the babysitter par excellence. In California there is a group called the 'Couch Potatoes', who consider themselves 'the true televisionaries'. They take their name from their favourite place for vegetating in front of the TV set and from the vegetable with many eyes. An advertisement to recruit members goes like this: 'Do you enjoy excessive amounts of TV viewing? Were some of the most enjoyable times of your life experienced in front of your set? Were your formative years nutured by the "electronic babysitter"? Are you annoyed by crybaby intellectuals who claim that TV viewing is counter-productive and a waste of time? Like to do most of your living on the couch?' — and so on.

Television has joined the family, the school, the peer group and the Church in providing a significant formative influence in the lives of young people. The television set has become an integral part of the household furniture. At present, young people in the developed countries watch an average of three hours television a day; twenty-one hours a week; 1,100 hours a year, 76,000 hours in a lifetime. That is the equivalent of eight years' continuous television viewing in a lifetime.

The television set has become, like the washing machine, the refrigerator, the electric iron, an everyday part of the modern household's essential equipment. In fact, it is no longer considered 'keeping up with the Joneses' to have two, or even three, television sets in the one household. The development of portable television sets means viewing need no longer be confined to the home. For instance, at a recent PGA Golf Tournament in Florida, a spectator in the stand at the eighteenth green remained glued to his portable TV, determined not to miss any action out on the course. With the advent of breakfast television and satellite viewing, watching television can become a twenty-four hours a day activity for the afficionado!

Television is the new 'pulpit in the skies' — millions of souls can be reached! Global links mean that souls on all four continents can be saved simultaneously by the one preacher! Television can even win elections, if American televangelist Jerry Falwell is to be believed. After the Reagan victory of 1980, the Moral Majority leader told a reporter: 'Church people are the secret ingredient that none of the pollsters counted on'. Closed circuit television means that today's farmer doesn't even have to attend his cows' calving or his sheeps' lambing. He can watch it all from the comfort of his electrically heated bed. Only an emergency demands his attention.

In some countries, television is seen as a tool of government. In 1966, the Irish Taoiseach (Prime Minister), Seán Lemass, stated in the Irish Parliament that 'RTE (the state radio and television service) was set up by legislation as an instrument of public policy, and as such, is responsible to the government. The government rejects the view that Radio Telefís Éireann should be, either generally or in regard to its current affairs and news programmes, completely independent of government supervision' (Desmond Fisher, *Broadcasting in Ireland*, Routledge & Kegan Paul, 1978, p. 32).

Italy is the only country in Europe which has fully deregulated television. For the past ten years, go-go girls and stripping housewives have punctuated commercials in over 600 local TV stations throughout the country. Only RAI, the national broadcasting company, which is funded from advertisements and licence fees, is allowed to operate nationally. However, through the local stations, major issues have been given a local perspective, frequently through the sweat of largely untried amateurs.

SATELLITE TECHNOLOGY

The advent of television over sixty years ago transformed our lifestyles. Here we go again! The second revolution in television has begun. Satellite television has arrived.

'We have blast off.' With these electrifying words from NASA Space Control Center, **Telstar 1** was launched in 1962. It was the world's first commercial communications satellite. This was followed by **Intelstat** which launched its first commercial communications satellite, **Early Bird**, in 1964. One of the first television broadcasts to be seen via satellite around the world was a programme called **Our World**, which featured the Beatles singing 'All you need is love', a song composed especially for the occasion. The telecast drew a worldwide audience of 160 million people, an astonishing achievement at the time. Now we have become blasé about satellite television. We have come to expect live pictures from around the world in sport, news, documentaries and current affairs programmes.

The mind-boggling advances in satellite technology and communications was illustrated on 24 January 1986, when an American satellite transmitted unedited images of an unknown world to the inhabitants of the planet earth. Thanks to the **Voyager 2** satellite, which had blasted off from the earth nearly ten years previously, we were three billion kilometres closer to the planet Uranus! It took two and three-quarter hours for the images of this distant place to reach the giant antennae of the receiving station in Australia. From there, the signals were relayed to Pasadena Center in California to be decoded and turned into images. Then they were distributed to newsrooms throughout the world via several geostationary satellites above the Atlantic, Indian and Pacific Oceans. This event, now forgotten by many, illustrates in the most vivid way possible the miracle of communications.

A communications satellite consists of three parts: the transmitter on the ground sends a signal to the satellite in space which receives it, amplifies it, switches it to a different frequency and transmits it back to earth, where it is received into a receiving dish and so to home, cable or TV station.

A satellite is like a radio transmitting tower, 22,000 miles tall, with its foundations at the equator. Satellites turn above our heads twenty-four hours a day. Rotating in the sky to the same rhythm as our globe rotates itself, these satellites appear to be 'fixed' or stationary, in relation to the earth's surface. That's why they are called geostationary. From its lofty perch above the world, each communications spacecraft transmits signals which cover entire continents — and beyond. A simple example illustrates this point. Suppose the earth is the hub of your bicycle,

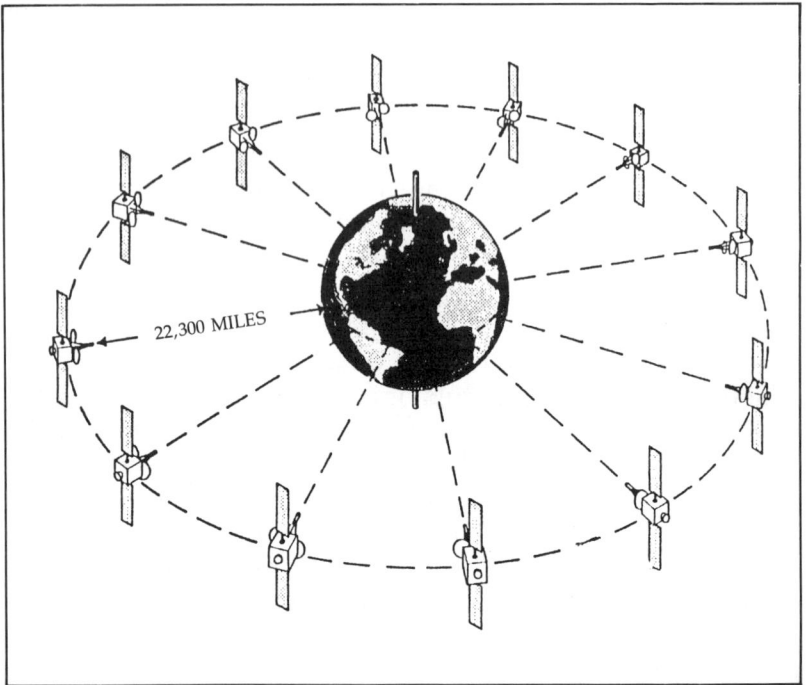

22,300 MILES

then the orbiting satellites are located at the end of the spokes of the wheel. With the rim, spokes and hub all continually moving at the same speed, their relationship remains unchanged. So a space-age band of satellite real estate straddles the globe. It is called the **Clarke Belt**, in honour of the man who first saw how artificial satellites could revolutionise worldwide communications.

Satellite signals can be plucked from the air through the use of a receiving dish. This saucer-like dish gathers the rather weak signal towards a focal point, strengthening them in the process. From the dish, the signal can be relayed into your home through cable. Up to quite recently, the dish required was quite large. It had to go in the garden rather than on the roof. However, it is envisaged that soon a satellite receiving dish can be built into the window of your home, much like a pane of glass. The suburban home in any upmarket American city will sport the satellite receiving dish and a swimming pool.

Sky Channel's satellite receiving dish.

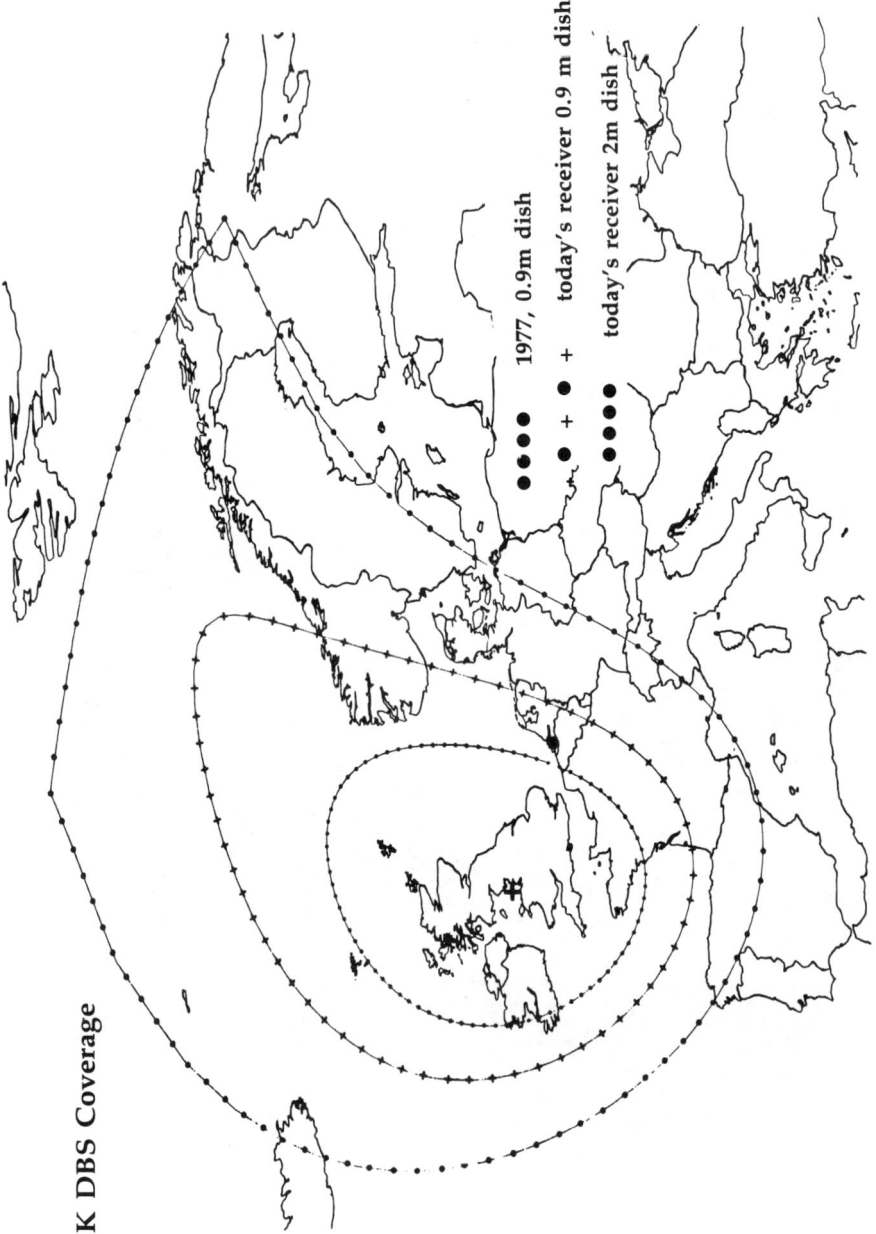

UK DBS Coverage

1977, 0.9m dish

today's receiver 0.9 m dish

today's receiver 2m dish

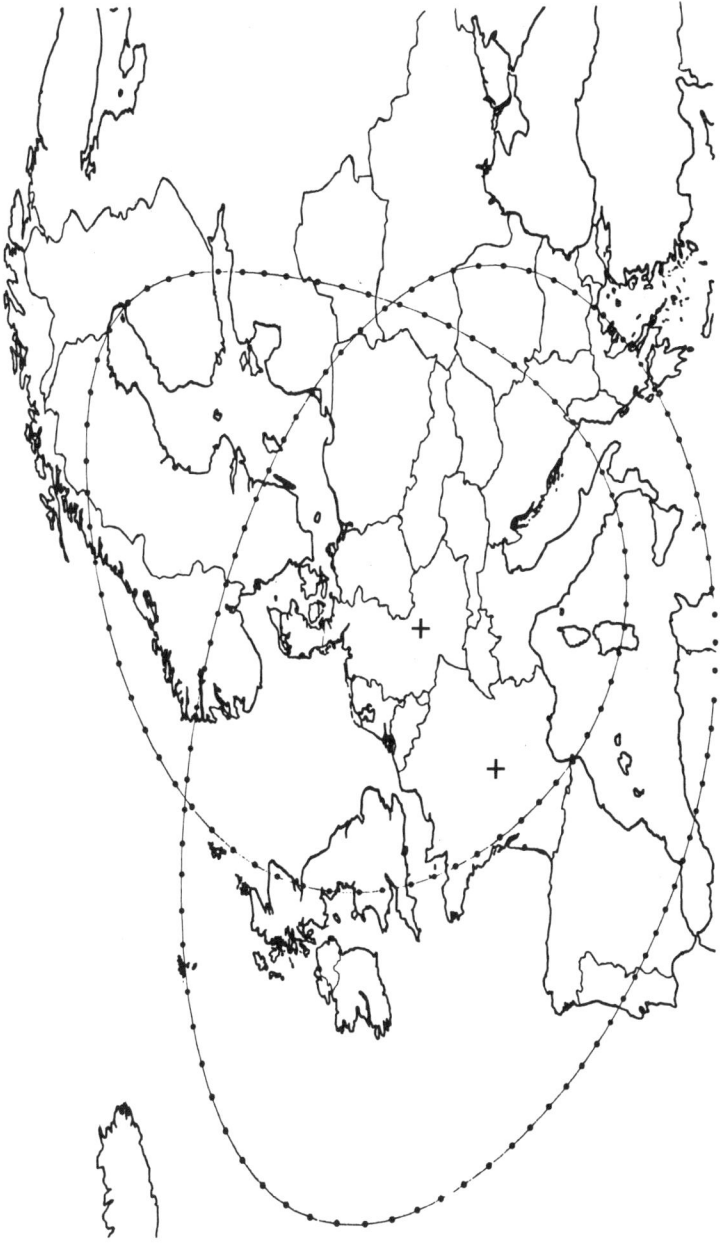

France & W. Germany

2m dish, today's receiver

The signals from the satellite can be scrambled or unscrambled. A scrambled signal is one that cannot be received without a decoder. This is a device to ensure that additional rental can be collected for additional channels received. Usually, hardcore pornography is on a scrambled signal which forces the customer to make the choice — do I want this trash or not?

Like radio, satellite transmission transcends national and international boundaries. The satellites observe the clouds and the tides (meteorological satellites), relay messages, data and images over long distances (telecommunications satellites), and broadcast television programmes (television satellites). Soon, there will be satellites from which one can take one's bearings or signal one's position with precision (navigation satellites).

Above: Three types of receiving aerials (dishes).
The white one on the left would have to be on a south facing wall and has to be pointed at the satellite. The fibreglass aerial on the right was made by the BBC Research Department. It's fibreglass, on a frame, and it is just sprayed with metal. The panel the girl is holding is the type of aerial that will eventually be used. It is the kind of thing that will be on your wall if the government does not prohibit satellite reception by individual householders.

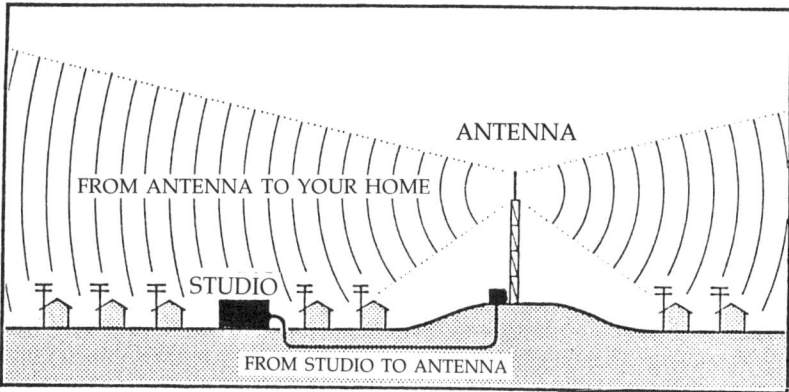

Before the advent of satellite or cable television the signals were received via an outdoor rooftop aerial.

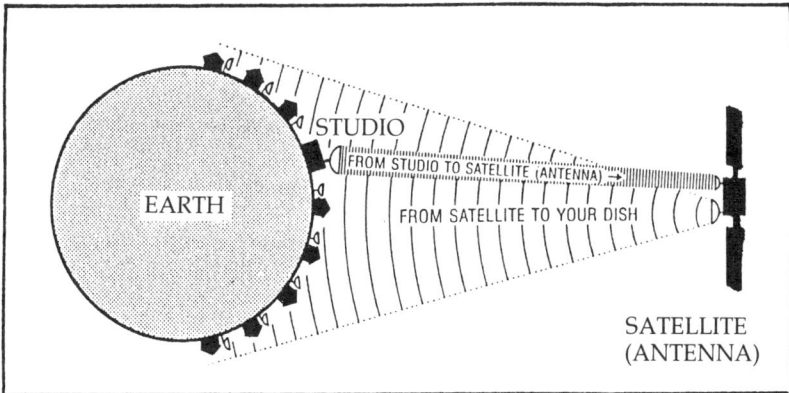

Satellite signals can be received directly (DBS).

The receiving area of the satellite is called a 'footprint' (see pp. 32-33). Again, the political, cultural and, indeed, religious implications of this are far-reaching.

CABLE TELEVISION
Cable television is a means of distributing the television signal through a cable from the point of distribution or a booster transmitter directly into the home of the receiver.

Almost all television in the Republic of Ireland is received via cable, through the state-owned **Cablelink Company**. Television reception evolved in this way through the takeover by the semi-state company of existing commercial companies. There was little national debate on the system of broadcasting adopted. People largely accepted the cable system on pragmatic grounds, because it eliminated the use of an external aerial and the quality of the reception was improved. The latter factor was important, due to the possibility of receiving good quality reception of four and now five channels originating in Britain.

In Britain on the other hand, a special enquiry under Lord Hunt was established 'to consider an expansion of cable systems which would permit cable to carry a wider range of entertainment and other services, but in a way consistent with the wider public interest, in particular the safeguarding of public service broadcasting'.

The very latest technological revolution in television is 'electronic news gathering' or **ENG**. Through the use of **ENG**, television news reporting has acquired all the immediacy and excitement formerly reserved for the 'on-the-spot' radio reporter. The replacement of celluloid film by videotape has cut out the delay formerly incurred by the need to process the film. Major news networks now have their own portable satellite earth stations. This allows reporters anywhere in the world to beam back **ENG** signals to their home base. Instant news joins all the other 'instants' that have changed the way we live.

THE VIDEO BOOM

The video tape recorder has already changed the way many people see television, liberating them from the tyranny of scheduling. They can now go out for the evening, and the episode of **Dallas** they would otherwise have missed is stored up and ready for viewing at any time. In many developed countries, every town and village has its video store where feature films, sport, cartoons and 'video nasties' are available for hire.

The potential of video has been discovered by industry, public relations and education. Cattle marts regularly feature video films advising farmers on animal care. The music industry relies to an increasing degree on video to sell its records and tapes. The **SKY** television satellite channel is a testimony to this fact. Educational videos have become a feature of academic life. The home video has replaced the 'holiday slides' as a record of family activities. Unfortunately, video has been widely used by entrepreneurial buccaneers to market pornography of the most disgusting kind.

Video games have appeared in amusement arcades and are used increasingly in the home. At the time of writing, video games in arcades are regarded in much the same way as the pool hall — rather shoddy, frequented by layabouts and a waste of money. But video games have a dynamic visual element. They are interactive. The game is not solely determined by the computer. It is very much influenced by the player's action.

On a tiny island about 2,000 miles from Jakarta in Indonesia, a headmaster complained that 'Everything was fine here until this evil video came to our village. Now my pupils start stealing coconuts and other things just to get hold of the money they need for the nightly performance. In school, of course, they are tired and fall asleep. And what is much worse, eight of my girls have become pregnant. As you know, these children, whatever they see on the screen, they try out themselves.' There is a price to be paid for progress.

In Sweden, concern for the video viewing habits of young people resulted in a survey of 11/15-year-olds in the town of Vaxjo (population 65,000). The results showed that young peole watch video cassettes with peers and largely in the absence of parents and siblings. While television tended to be a family-based activity, video clearly had a group-oriented character. Among the 15-year-olds, only 2% watched video with their parents, as opposed to 77% who watched it with friends.

The women of Gujarat, India, demonstrated another use for video. The municipal authorities planned to turn their street market into a car park. A video, shown to the Municipal Commissioner, demonstrated the injustice of this planning decision. The result was the provision of an even better market for the women. The *Hindustan Times* reported: 'This bit of modern technology has allowed normally powerless and voiceless people to articulate their concerns, reach an audience from which they are usually cut off and become part of a decision-making process in a major Indian city.'

Video in itself is neutral as a means of communication. It can be used for good or evil. By now most people are familiar with the proliferation of pornography through video. Ruedi Hofmann, in *Group Media Journal*, published by Sonolux, Germany, gives a particularly sad example of the misuse of video. He writes: 'One of my students at the major seminary made a small-scale research on video habits among high school students in the city of Yogyakarta. He was able to collect enough confidential information to get down to the following facts. At the Catholic high school where he conducted the research, there was a clandestine club of students who put together their pocket money to obtain pornographic video cassettes. They were provided by a lady in the port city of Semarang, 120 kilometers from Yogyakarta. The students travelled to Semarang by turns to get new cassettes and to bring back the old ones. Whenever the parents of the one of the club's members spent the night away from home, this was the opportunity for the club to meet and watch so-called "blue films".'

GROWTH CURVE OF VIDEO SALES

	1979	1986
Western Europe	841,000	34 million
North America	1 million	45 million
Asia	1 million	31 million

Penetration of Video Cassette Recorders (VCRs) into families

	1986
Oman	89%
United Arab Emirates	83%
Kuwait	73%
Singapore	65%
Qatar	62%

Lebanon	62%
Iceland	62%
Israel	60%
Bahrain	58%
Hong Kong	57%
Malaysia	50%
Australia	50%
Panama	46%
India	43%
Japan	43%
United States	43%
Philippines	42%
China	1.9%
USSR	0.1%

Since 1975, two video tape recorders have dominated the market, the Betamax of Sony and the VHS of Japan Victor Company (JVC). The two are incompatible. A BETA tape will not play on a VHS and vice versa.

Popularity of systems

	VHS		BETA
Ireland	97%	Ecuador	90%
Brazil	95%	Peru	85%
Finland	90%	Venezuela	80%
Hong Kong	90%	Colombia	60%
Singapore	90%		
Japan	85%		
United States	85%		
Australia	85%		
France	85%		
Germany	80%		
Belgium	80%		
Canada	80%		
New Zealand	80%		
Sweden	80%		

Top borrowers/buyers of video cassettes

Irish	75%
Germans	70%
Greeks	70%
Norwegians	70%
Finns	65%
Dutch	50%
Swedes	50%

Note: In Great Britain, the owners of VCRs buy or borrow one cassette a week.

The Irish Video Market

1.	19% of all adults rent 5 videos per month on average		
2.	Adult population (those 16+ years)		2,520,000
3.	19% of 2,520,000	=	478,000
4.	X 60 (5 x 12) videos per year	=	28,728,000
5.	Average cost per night per rental		£1.25
6.	**Total market value**		**£35,910,000**
7.	Adult market segment		£7,223,000
8.	'Family' market		£25,137,000
9.	Legitimate market		£17,750,000
10.	Surplus (counterfeit revenue)		£10,937,000
11.	150,000 video cassettes per year are distributed illegally and are pirated copies primarily of the counterfeit type.		

There are different video colour standards used in different parts of the world. This means, in effect, that without transferring the tape to the prevailing colour standard in our country or acquiring a VCR of that standard, you will be unable to view the tape. The American system is called NTSC. The system used in French speaking countries, the USSR and some other countries is SECAM (see chart below). The PAL system is used in England

and English-speaking Africa, Oceania and some other countries listed below. This is important because tourists and visitors purchase videos in America, not realising that they will be unable to view them in Europe without paying to have them converted, or seeking out one of the very few NTSC videos available.

In January 1983, the cover of *Time* magazine featured not the usual Man of the Year, but an illustration of the Machine of the

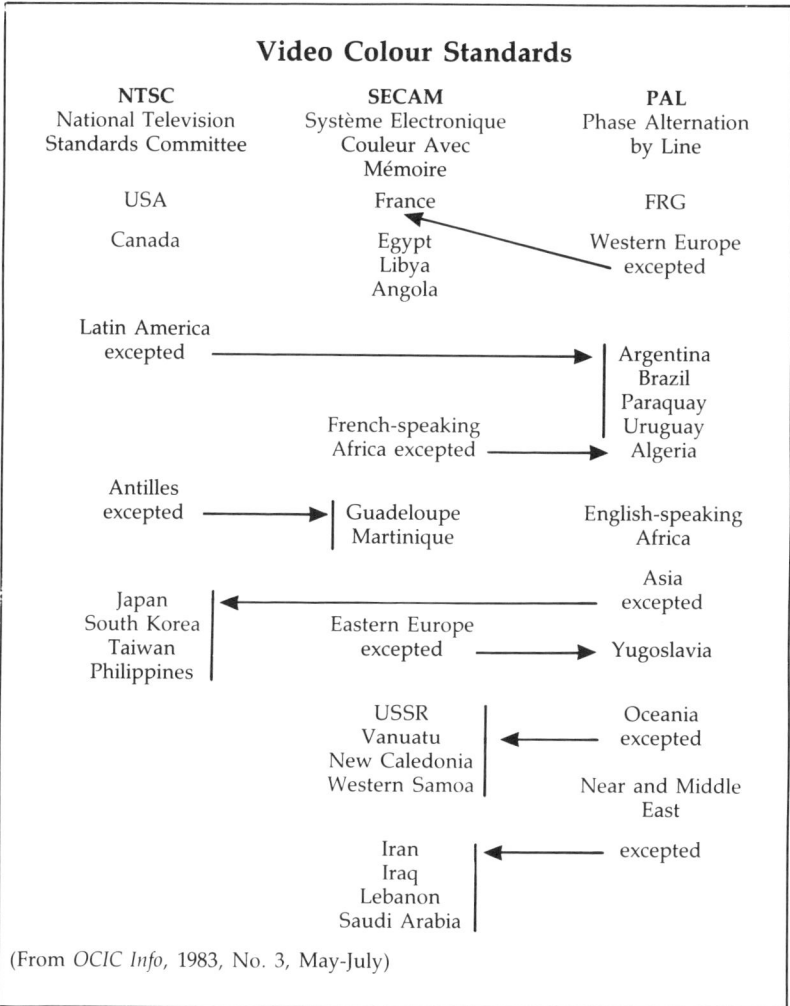

Video Colour Standards

NTSC	SECAM	PAL
National Television Standards Committee	Système Electronique Couleur Avec Mémoire	Phase Alternation by Line
USA	France	FRG
Canada	Egypt Libya Angola	Western Europe excepted
Latin America excepted		Argentina Brazil Paraguay Uruguay Algeria
	French-speaking Africa excepted	
Antilles excepted	Guadeloupe Martinique	English-speaking Africa
Japan South Korea Taiwan Philippines	Eastern Europe excepted	Asia excepted Yugoslavia
	USSR Vanuatu New Caledonia Western Samoa	Oceania excepted Near and Middle East
	Iran Iraq Lebanon Saudi Arabia	excepted

(From *OCIC Info*, 1983, No. 3, May-July)

Year: the personal computer. The fact that the prestigious Man of the Year award went to a machine illustrates in a dramatic fashion how, in a few short years, the PC has entered the lives, offices, homes and schools of the average American. According to *Time*, the 'greatest influence for good or evil' in 1982 was the computer. In the popular imagination, the computer is more than a mere machine; it is a potent force actively shaping our social and private lives.

CALCULATORS AND COMPUTERS

The message sent by Samuel Morse when he opened the United States' first telegraph line in 1844 was a question: 'What hath God wrought?'

Some were enthusiastic about the possibilities of the new invention. They saw it as a gift from God that would help to build up the community and foster brotherhood and sisterhood between people. Then, as today, the entrepreneurs saw its commercial possibilities. They were interested in the possibilities of exploiting the new technology for profit. Some were sceptical and unwilling to be impressed. They would have preferred things to remain the same. Naturally, the military possibilities were noted. Today the computer elicits the same reaction except, of course, that God is seldom referred to.

Robots have become commonplace in industry. However, seeing one in the street without visible human control is still a cause for raised eyebrows. A maverick robot was arrested in Beverley Hills in 1982! The four-foot robot was hauled off to the police cells when it was unable to give an account of itself as it strode, lights flashing, along the exclusive Beverley Hills Drive in Los Angeles. A policeman was called to the scene, and when the robot failed to respond to questioning he was taken down to the station. The policeman said, 'The device was operated by remote control, but the operator refused to come forward and identify himself — so the robot is spending the night in the station.'

Calculators, at first unwieldy, then pocket-sized, replaced the mathematical tables in the classroom and the office. As I write, I carry in my pocket a wafer thin 'calling card'. It can store 3,000 characters, addresses, names and telephone numbers, whatever you fancy, all available for instant retrieval. At the same time, it doubles as a pocket calculator. Its weight is measured in ounces! One must ask whether computerisation on a massive scale diminishes creative thinking. The danger is that increased technology will be seen as having a solution to all our problems. Just as medicine proposes 'a pill for every ill', technology may suggest that the answer lies in the machine.

West German engineers claim to have removed one of the biggest obstacles to the automation of factories; they have built robots which can select objects from a muddle in a box without human help. Researchers at Siemens claim that the new system can recognise sixty-eight different shapes, overlapping by up to 20% under varying illuminations. The device takes between 0.5 and 2.5 seconds to identify objects, depending on their complexity.

And how about this example from the information age:

> Michael Ducross, a gentle Canadian-born Indian, took an illegal left turn one day on his way home from the grocery store. He waited while the policeman checked with the local station over his two-way radio. The clerk in Huntington, California, keyed the details into his computer, flashing a request for information to Sacramento. Nothing showed up. Three thousand miles away, however, in Washington's National Crime Information Center, the FBI's computerised records showed that Michael Ducross had gone absent without leave from the Marine Corps — ten years earlier.
>
> He landed up in jail for five months before it was discovered that, in fact, he had obtained a discharge under a special programme for foreign citizens and native Americans. (David Lyon, *The Silicon Society*, Lion Publishing, p. 97).

THE PRINT MEDIA ARE AFFECTED BY THE TECHNOLOGICAL REVOLUTION

The grandfather of the mass circulation paper in Britain, Lord Northcliffe, died in 1922 at the age of fifty-six, an insane millionaire. His life had been devoted to the newspaper industry.

Yet, if Northcliffe were alive today and paid a visit to the editorial offices of one of Britain's newest mass circulation newspapers he would be ill at ease.

Today, Britain's first fully electronic newspaper, pioneered by the mercurial Eddie Shah, is the newspaper revolution in practice, with printing at four separate plants around the country and with no composing room. Advertising and editorial content of the newspaper is prepared by the use of 'state of the art' electronic integrated text, while graphics and photographic handling systems are transmitted simultaneously to four regional print centres. Eddie Shah shattered all the traditions hitherto considered sacrosanct. He chose Pimlico rather than Fleet Street, he chose colour rather than monochrome, he negotiated no-strike agreements in an industry riddled with industrial guerrilla warfare, he chose technology rather than human labour. We now know he didn't succeed, but that's another story.

In Japan, the newspaper *Ashai Simbun* has installed a computer system which transfers newsprint to the presses, photosets the print, automatically bales the 12,000,000 copies in the required numbers for each district of the country and loads them on to waiting lorries; all without the intervention of a single human being.

THE EFFECTS OF THE COMMUNICATIONS REVOLUTION

There is little agreement among learned commentators regarding the effects of the new media explosion on people's lives. In fact, diametrically opposed views are held with equal conviction.

Dr Hans Flore, until recently the General Secretary of the World Association for Christian Communication, is of the view that what we are experiencing is an upheaval of massive proportions.

> It is not enough to call what we are experiencing 'rapid social change' or even 'revolution', since these connote only social or political upheaval. The change is more basic in that it modifies everything we have known before. Arend van Leewen suggests that there have been only two basic eras in all of history. The first is the autocratic era, in which we

have lived until now. Always before, human society has apprehended life as a cosmic totality, where belief in a god or gods outside human experience held together the contradictory and confusing elements of the human community. But relatively suddenly, within the last 300 years, we have moved away from this unifying concept into a multiform system of relationships, with no specific cornerstone, no single integrating element that gives all other things their reason for being. We have moved into the Technological Era, and this is the great new fact of our time. The communications revolution, the Age of Information, the Information Society — these are under way in every aspect of life (*The Myth of the Information Revolution*, edited by Michael Traber, Sage Publications, p. 127).

Another commentator confirms the view held by Dr Flore. In *A Vision All Can Share*, published by the United Catholic Conference, the view is put forward that the ongoing revolution 'has and is affecting even the basic structures of American society. This bloodless, nearly unobtrusive revolution was nothing less than a major transition in the way Americans began to see and understand themselves in an affluent, highly mobile, increasingly college educated and mass mediated society. The primary agent of change, television, dominated the mass media, altering the roles of other media and America's basic institutions.'

On the other hand, some feel that everything changes and everything remains the same. Michael Traber, editor of the journal *Media Development*, feels that the new 'revolution' is simply consolidating the old order. In *The Myth of the Information Revolution* he argues that the communications revolution, rather than liberating us, has been an exercise in consolidating the military, economic and political power of the elite. Information is power, and it is also a commodity to be bought and sold. It has been estimated that 50% of all trans-border data flow takes place with the communications networks of individual transnational corporations. Add to this the transborder data flow that takes place within the military and foreign services and you have a closed sky — what Traber calls an 'information implosion' rather than explosion, all sealed and contained within a corporate world of secrecy.

The McBride Report, *Many Voices, One World*, pointed out that rather than benefiting from the information revolution through a free-flow of information, we have a 'one-way flow'. Data messages, media programmes, cultural products, are usually directed from bigger to smaller countries, from those with power and technological means towards those less advanced, from the developed to the developing world and, on a national level, from the power centre downwards.

In general, people are unaware of the degree to which their view of reality is presented to them by the media. McLuhan coined a less familiar phrase — 'the medium is the message'. The effects of media are not perceptible immediately. It takes a major trauma even to begin to ask the question — What, if any, are the effects of the mass media on our thoughts and behaviour?

When Michael Ryan stalked the streets of the quiet English market town of Hungerford with guns blazing, commentators began to look for the Rambo connection. Sylvester Stallone really was walking the streets in combat fatigues and headband. It took sixteen deaths and bitter agony before the possible effects of media violence and human behaviour were examined. Most likely, Rambo videos were freely available without comment in Hungerford's video rental stores.

Eric McLuhan, son of the late Marshall McLuhan, believes that the very nature of TV itself has bred a new kind of person who cannot sustain long-term commitments. TV, with its multiple choices and promises of instant gratification, trains people to the short term. He fears for the future of the family, which depends on long-term commitment to spouse and child. Once viewing has become habitual, it is unlikely that the family will have the capacity effectively to evaluate what they are watching.

Apart from television, the computer provokes questions about what it means to be human. Will robots eventually dispense with us altogether? The concept appears to belong to the realms of science fiction, and yet it is not at all as fanciful as it seems. According to a 1972 London conference on computing, Japan is engaged in an all-out effort to construct machines that will be more intelligent than people. An 'electronic Pearl Harbour' was feared, spearheaded by machines that would be able to see, hear, talk, recognise individual human faces and 'think'.

Where modern technology is concerned, the Churches tend to take a pragmatic view. The dominant question is, how can we use this new invention to increase our effectiveness? The Churches concern themselves with the practical problems of buying and installing and administering computer systems or video or television. They are in danger of becoming immersed in the computer age without understanding its more profound implications. This means that individual Churchpeople, if they are interested in the media at all, adopt a critical approach to this or that particular programme which offends their Christian values. The question is not how the modern means of communications can be harnessed in the service of the Gospel. That may be just a matter of resources and expertise. The pervasive world of modern technology is having some effect on people's lives, not just on the way they live, but on their perspective on the deeper questions of life and death and the mysteries of faith. Religious education has to take account of the degree to which young people are subjected to other singers singing different songs. For Churchpeople, involved on a day-to-day basis with Church activities, the communications revolution may appear peripheral to the deeper questions of life. But for many of their parishioners working in industry, medicine, banking or government, technology is conquering hitherto unsurmountable obstacles, so that it can be difficult to reconcile the claims of faith with the remarkable advances in communications and technology. People are irritated by the impossibility of subjecting the claims of faith to empirical analysis. The concept of faith as a 'supernatural gift' received through Baptism is far removed from teletext and viewdata and satellites and video.

Chapter Three

Media in the Service of the Gospel

In one pithy sentence, John the Evangelist wrote, 'God is love'. In fact, the Trinity is a *community* of love. So often God is characterised as our Orwellian 'Big Brother', watching us daily with furrowed brow, chalking up our indiscretions. If God is love, a community of love, then his love is active. It is a bustling, thrusting activity that reaches out to embrace and enfold others. Seminarians, while still wet behind the ears, learn *'bonum est diffusivum sui'*. In down to earth language, 'goodness or love seeks always to spread itself out'. The poet Francis Thompson pictured God as a lover in pursuit of the beloved: 'I fled him down the days and down the nights...'. The communication of love as part of the very life of God in the Trinity and as central to God's purpose as creator and redeemer is pivotal to the mission of the Church. Is it possible to imagine a God who has no interest in communicating with his creation? If it is, Christianity becomes irrelevant. Communication is a two-way process that takes place between those sharing a common nature, hence the Incarnation. God, in the mystery of redemption, communicates and demonstrates his love in sending Jesus who was 'born in the likeness of men'.

God's plan of redemption included calling men and women out of estrangement into communion with one another. The 'love one another' call of Jesus is a call to community.

The Church then is the community of those who believe in Christ as God's communicator. It is also called to be the visible sign of God's universal love. The Church is called to live out the unlimited communication of God's love, reconciliation and wholeness to the world. The Church fails insofar as it doesn't succeed in presenting to the world, through word and practical action, the true face of God's love. Fr Avery Dulles has pointed out that communication is at the very heart of what the Church is — a vast communications network calling people out of estrangement into communion. There is no Church without communication.

The Church has the commission from Christ to be God's witness in 'Jerusalem, Judaea, Samaria and throughout the world'. In the past the common language system of the Roman Empire, the relative ease of travel on the Roman roads, and the diaspora of the Jews facilitated the spread of the Good News of God's love and redemption through the passion, death and resurrection of Jesus. In fulfilling this commission, the 'message' is always quite decisively affected by the dominant technology of the day. For instance, what is probably the oldest bit of New Testament writing, dating possibly from the year 94 AD, is a scrap of St John's Gospel, written on papyrus and known as the John Rylands Greek Papyrus. Papyrus was a kind of paper made from a reed that grew in the delta of the Nile and it was then the most modern and suitable material for the communication of the message, 'God is love'.

Later the Gospels and the commentaries on them were written on animal hide, staked out, dried, stretched and rubbed clean. The next breakthrough was to thin, wax-coated wood, which was later replaced by parchment and the first book became a reality.

In the sixteenth century, it was Martin Luther who exploited the recently invented printing press, to indulge in an orgy of pamphleteering that unleashed a flood of religious tracts throughout Germany. The number of tracts issued in Germany in the years 1521-24, exceeds the quantity issued during any other period of four years in German history until today. On average, Luther wrote a major tract or treatise every two weeks of his life — not to mention the publication of sermons and university lectures.

The commission received from Christ to 'go therefore, teach all nations', places on the Church the responsibility of making God known and loved, and availing of the best possible means of doing so. In addition the Church, as I said, is 'the community of those who believe in Christ'. The building of a community demands effective communications. Industrialists spend vast amounts of money, not only on advertising their products, but also on building up a harmonious work-force. They know that this will pay off in increased production, increased sales and increased profits.

The Church is committed to communicating God's love through work and example. Authentic communication is participatory. This is a challenge for a body unused to participatory communication. Genuine communication cannot take place in a climate of division, alienation, isolation — all of which prevent social interaction. Effective communication within the Church is going to be one of the greatest challenges to the future of the Church and the future well-being of the Church will depend to an increased degree on the effectiveness of her internal communications. Obviously, extensive papal travels, episcopal synods and commissions, national conferences of bishops and parish councils are having some effect, albeit peripheral as yet, on internal communications within the Church.

I often get the impression that Church leaders behave in a manner which implies that 'we have the Holy Spirit with us and it really doesn't matter how we are treated by the media', or that 'our appointment is from God and therefore we have no obligation to explain ourselves to those within or without the Church'. This attitude, where it exists, is in direct contradiction of the Vatican's most heavyweight document on the media.

> As representatives of the Church, bishops, priests, religious and laity are increasingly asked to write in the press, or appear on radio and television, or to collaborate in filming. They are warmly urged to undertake this work, which has consequences far more important than is usually imagined. (*Communio et Progressio*, 1. n. 106).

When will we ever learn that participatory communication gives people a new sense of dignity, a new experience of community?

THE CHURCH IS AFFECTED BY THE MEDIA

Last September I took a cab from downtown San Francisco to the nearby Jesuit University. It was two weeks prior to the Pope's visit. Unprompted by me, the cabbie asked 'What do you think of the Pope coming to visit?' This was the start of a discussion on Catholics, the Pope, the complexity of Catholic doctrine. He ended by saying, 'I don't really have any religion. I try to live by good old Shakespeare "to thine own self be true". I don't know much about Catholics, except what I read in the papers.' The cabbie was just one of countless millions worldwide for whom their view of the Church and its personnel and activities is mediated and moulded by the popular media. The David Yallops, Malachi Martins, Andrew Greeleys and the *Daily Mirror*, together with the Frank Carsons, Gay Byrnes and Terry Wogans, whether we like it or not, do more to project a view of the Church than do the Vatican or mitred prelates.

The Church is news, trivial at times, like an article in the *San Francisco Chronicle* detailing the eating habits of the Pope and the possible meals that would be provided during his forthcoming visit. The Church and its personnel are increasingly the focus of media hype. For instance, the Pope has made the cover of *Time* magazine on five occasions. Cover stories headed 'John Paul Superstar' and 'Discord in the Church' have made available information about the Catholic Church from Michigan Avenue in Chicago to Dalhousie Square in Calcutta. *Newsweek* has also featured Pope John Paul on its cover on two occasions. When Mehmet Ali Agca fired the shot that wounded him on 13 May 1981, the news had spread throughout the world within minutes. Troubles in the Vatican, like the Marcinkus affair, can no longer be kept within the family. The worldwide travels of the Pope have highlighted the Church's profile internationally. The universal media take great delight in revealing the cracks and inconsistencies in the Church, inconsistencies that demand explanation! On the other hand, the same media can be used to demonstrate the unity of faith and charity of which the Church is capable. The acres of newsprint and the many television hours devoted to the work of Mother Teresa are an example.

As the communications industry continues to expand and the world we live in contracts, it appears inevitable that it will be a world and a future shaped to an enormous extent by the electronic media. We desperately need to bring together what we already know or can project about the telecommunications revolution as it will affect human life, society and the world order. As Karl Rahner has pointed out, we need a futurology of the Church.

There are many impressive examples of Church personnel using the modern means of communications in the service of the Gospel. Many of these witnesses come from the developing world where, in my experience, there is greater sensitivity to the potential of modern technology in the apostolate. Some time ago, I was delivering a talk to a group of priests in the first world. I decided to use an overhead projector to illustrate what I had to say. One priest, of recent vintage, exclaimed, 'Aren't you wonderful to be able to use that machine — I wouldn't know how to put in the plug.'

The Church will always need the preachers and teachers, the catechists and social healers — even the bishops — to do a job well. But, in the information age, the job can be done even more effectively when we learn how to claim the available technology and media in the service of the Kingdom. Can Churchpeople huddle in a bunker and ignore the realities which, for others, are opportunities? That is one reason why this book is being written!

The following random examples will give you some idea of the possibilities being explored at local level by people of initiative.

Neira, a Paraguayan priest, has a tough assignment, far removed from media or technology of any sort. His mission in the Paraguayan jungle has no electricity. On a trip to North America, Fr Neira was introduced to the marvels of video. He was shown simple films that would help him to explain the Gospel message. He received a gift of a video recorder. Off Fr Neira went, with the video recorder strapped to his mule. He was full of enthusiasm and excitement, anticipating the reaction of the villagers to this new and wonderful invention. I know what you are thinking! No electricity! Neira had acquired two solar panels, roughly the size of a biscuit tin. They were enough to charge batteries for two hours of video viewing.

Mother Angelica, a Franciscan Sister of the traditional wing of the American Catholic Church was invited to participate in a TV chat show. That same night the station was to screen a pornographic movie. Mother Angelica saw an opportunity to strike a bargain. She would do the chat show if the station removed the film from their schedule. It didn't work! Mother Angelica thought 'Well, if they can broadcast, so can I'. She returned to her convent, converted the garage into a miniscule studio and started broadcasting. Today, a convent nestling into the hills in a suburb of Birmingham, Alabama, boasts of a huge satellite 'link-up' dish in the back garden, and **Mother Angelica Live** is broadcast coast-to-coast in the United States. I was privileged to receive the hospitality of Mother Angelica and be shown around the impressive studios that were built on faith and prayer. Mother Angelica is one of those exceptional people who recognised the potential of the communications revolution and was determined that the energy unleashed could and would be harnessed for the proclamation of the Gospel. According to Mother Angelica, 'Unless we are willing to do the ridiculous, God will not do the miraculous.'

In Australia, one priest has used technology to reach young people. Fr Jim McLaren of Sydney, Australia, is the disc jockey for an extremely popular phone-in and music radio programme for young people. He has been successful in reaching many of the lonely and alienated, by combining a friendly, non-judgmental style with their favourite Top Forty songs. Through his work with the Catholic Communications Centre, McLaren has developed his ministry to youth from an initial series of seven-minute programmes to a full four-hour Sunday night programme, **Cross Talk**. He regularly handles about forty-five phone calls and fourteen music tracks each evening. About 70% of the potential teenage audience listen regularly to **Cross Talk**. They have a chance to talk with him and hear their peers discuss real life events in which they are also interested. They feel free to talk about anything — drugs, leisure activities, records — and to ask questions about religion and relationships.

Shortly after his **Jesus of Nazareth** was broadcast, Zeffirelli was asked to visit a parish on his vacation route. After some hesitation he arrived, to find five teenagers just about to be baptised. They found Christ through Zeffirelli's film, a Christ never mentioned by their parents. Troubled at their neglect, they had gone to the priest, received instruction and were now being baptised. The media had done for these young people what neither the families, out of ignorance, nor the Church, through lack of contact, had been able to do. (As told in *Research Trends in Religious Communications*, vol. 5, no. 1).

In most parishes, the potential of the media as an instrument of evangelisation has hardly been recognised. Many wealthy parishes do not possess a video, a common enough piece of electronic furniture in the homes of a great number of parishioners. Is video for the affluent? Any morning in a soulless suburb of Dublin, one crippled by unemployment, the video store is one of the first ports of call. A local priest told me, 'It is not unusual for an unemployed person to rent out three videos for the day. These videos will be passed from house to house, in a roster, during the twenty-four hour rental period. For some it means getting out of bed at an ungodly hour.'

RADHARC

The longest running programme on Irish television is called **Radharc**. For twenty-five years it has enjoyed a consistently high level of popularity. Archbishop McQuaid, once referred to as 'the grey eminence', had the foresight to assign Fr Joe Dunn to undertake a television course run by ABC, one of the independent television companies based in Manchester. Fr Joe became Ireland's first 'television priest', before the country had its own station. The foresight of the Archbishop prevailed even further when Fr Joe and a diocesan colleague, Fr Des Forristal, were sent on a three month course at the Academy of Broadcasting Arts in New York. This was in 1959, pre-Conciliar days! The outstanding success of the **Radharc** series meant that a religious dimension has always been part of the output of the Irish television service.

One of the success stories of the Catholic Communications Institute of Ireland has been the Veritas Video Productions unit. With a full-time team of five and its own production facilities, the team produces ten/twelve hour-long videos a year. The subject matter of the videos is pastoral. Parish-based programmes for Baptism, Confirmation, training lay readers and special ministers of the Eucharist, are among the videos produced. In addition, the video department 'buys in' the most professionally produced foreign material and makes it available through a catalogue, which now lists well over 200 videos. Sales of over 800 videos a month mean that Veritas videos now reach most parts of the English-speaking Catholic world. This is an operation which is completely self-funding.

In a Dublin secondary school, over 90% of the 160 pupils in their final year, in answer to the question — 'When do you listen to the radio?' replied 'When I wake up in the morning'. Their first conscious action was to plug in the radio. Many of the same students also said that they listened to the radio in bed at night. Despite the pervasiveness of the mass media, a series of media textbooks, *Introduction to the Mass Media* and *Understanding the Mass Media*, aimed at informing secondary school pupils on the media, failed to achieve the response one would have expected in a media saturated society. At the level of the secondary school pupil, little attention is paid to examining and critically evaluating the media. The same is true in seminaries.

I was at a meeting recently when a reputable parish priest complained bitterly about the innumerable demands that are made on the parish clergy. Liturgists demand a level of excellence Sunday after Sunday from the clergy. Catechists expect them to be fully informed on religious education. The diocesan social services demand involvement in areas of social concern and the youth services claim that their initiatives must take priority, as the youth of today is the Church of tomorrow. The media buff is one more voice claiming the attention of harassed parish clergy.

How many pastoral workers involved in parish life will have the competence or initiative to learn about liturgy, catechetics or youth ministry? A small number. On the other hand the overwhelming majority will read a daily paper or tune into the radio or watch the television for at least a few moments a day. They are media consumers. My plea is not that they attempt to become experts but that they become conscious of the potential that the media has for spreading the word of God. I have given a few examples of this potential in this chapter. The hardware and software are available and they are 'user friendly', to use a horrible cliché. I feel the task is not one of acquiring enormous expertise or information but of acquiring the motivation to use what is already available.

Chapter Four

The Pastor in the Television Age

What are the implications of the communications revolution for the pastor, lay or clerical? Formerly, the man-of-the-cloth had the stage all to himself. The communication was one way and it was moralistic and frequently amateurish in style and delivery. Here was the voice of reason and orthodoxy, delivering a message that was unchallenged. Not so any more.

Nobody who looks at a television screen and sees millions of Muslims prepared to face 'martyrdom' in a holy war with Iraq can remain unimpressed by their religious motivation. Television is presenting a plurality of faiths with impartiality. It is revealing the fact that Christianity isn't the unchallenged world faith we vaguely thought it was thirty or forty years ago. This places increased demands on the preacher in terms of reason and conviction.

Television challenges the faith of viewers. How does one reconcile the all-loving God with the multitudes of Ethiopians pathetically facing inevitable death from starvation in a world of plenty? How about the Colombian earthquake which killed thousands, some before our eyes on the television screen? Television discussions involving obviously intelligent people who dismiss the claims of Christianity force us to re-evaluate our faith and choose to accept it rather than take it for granted as we did in the past.

Dr Colin Morris, in a talk to Christian media personnel in May 1987, presented the challenge like this:

The greatest ecumenical occasion on earth was the marriage of Prince Charles and Princess Di. Twelve million people watched, the greatest congregation ever assembled on earth saw it the moment it took place, from the steppes of Russia to the southernmost tip of Latin America. All twelve million saw it together! An even bigger occasion will be the next Olympics in Korea when probably 200 million people will see the Games as they happen. We are being driven into a kind of headlong ecumenicity which forces us to have certain perspectives about the dimensions of the world's problems. How high on the agenda of the whole inhabited earth is the question of whether the Anglican Church ordains women priests? Now there is premature ecumenicity which is putting all our problems and all our challenges on a quite different scale.

The pastor cannot ignore the global scale of the media. He too must get inside the skins, so to speak, of his listeners, as television is so adept at doing. His ear has to be finely tuned to the cries of the hearts of people. The gospel he preaches has to be proclaimed against the perspective of the Television Age. Recently, a parish priest of my acquaintance mounted a pulpit to preach on the Immaculate Conception with a sermon dated 1928 tucked under his arm!

Media personnel have to be real professionals to survive in a tough, competitive world. The survivors have mastered the art of communication. The preacher does not have to be in competition but surely he occasionally needs to thin out his vocabulary and speak intelligibly. A friend of mine, a high-flier, lives in a rural part of Ireland. His job takes him abroad nearly weekly. As a convinced Christian he explained his recurring disappointment to me as he sat week after week listening to 'drivel' from his local pulpit. He sought an interview with the pastor to discuss his desire for some kind of weekly spiritual nourishment. The man admitted that he seldom prepared a sermon with any degree of diligence and apologised. He didn't realise that some of his parishioners were in Bangkok or New York or London that week. Global travel as well as global communication places an added responsibility on the preacher.

Global business travel, forced or voluntary emigration, mass tourism, have implications for the pastor. A recent AIDS advertising campaign aimed exclusively at the business traveller began 'when you're on your own abroad and you've just finished a tough day, you feel you deserve something more exciting than bed with a good book...'. The campaign will be followed by a similar one aimed at tourists. Rapid physical communication means that it is impossible not to be exposed to standards hostile to the gospel message. Solidly religious societies are fragmenting because for the first time in recent history people are being exposed to peoples with different values, cultures and religious standards. The popular tourist areas of the world tolerate and facilitate a level of promisicuous behaviour that confronts and challenges the believing Christian. Even highly graded hotels will provide pornographic video entertainment for their guests. The preacher, to be effective, has to take account of these societal changes.

In a questionnaire to a group of 128 seventeen-year-old schoolgirls, I asked — 'What rules are there about TV in your family?' 83% answered, 'None'. In other words, indiscriminate viewing was the order of the day. These same young people will sit in the pews on Sunday.

After a few months in the seminary the Professor of Homiletics called the first year students together. He asked us to draw up a fictional biography of a composite typical parishioner. This was not to be 'just a few lines' but rather a complete biographical sketch of several foolscap pages. Even though it is now over thirty years since I completed that exercise every detail of the 'character' I chose remains with me to this day.

'Mary White' was a twenty-five-year-old secretary. She loved dancing. Saturday night was her night 'on the town'. She seldom arrived home before two in the morning. She generally attended last Mass on Sunday, which in those days was a midday Mass. There were five in the family, excluding her mother and father. Her father, a van driver, left the task of rearing the children to 'Mammy', as was usual then. Mary was not a sports lover but enjoyed popular light music. She had a regular boyfriend, Jimmy, whom she liked and thought that he might some day ask her to marry him. This is only the bare bones of the story but Mary haunted me for the next six years of my training.

'What's the name of your character?' barked the homiletics professor. 'What time did she go to bed at last night'? Then he would go for the jugular — 'Do you think that Mary, who was dancing in a smoke-filled ballroom to loud music until the early hours of the morning, would have the remotest idea of what you are talking about?' Or he would ask: 'What magazines does Mary read every week?' I would sheepishly reel off the names of the women's magazines Mary would be most likely to read. The killer punch would then be delivered. 'Would Mary understand the words you are using in that sermon?'

This was the most valuable exercise in my whole training for the priesthood. We were trained to get right into the skins of those to whom we would later preach the Gospel. We were challenged to listen and think and observe the people and the world around us. Today's vocabulary is significantly different from what it was thirty years ago. Today's Mary will be using a word processor, travelling to Portugal or even China for her holidays, going to discos instead of dances, watching television and using a bank card and perhaps reading a tabloid daily newspaper. Has the thinking and vocabulary of the preacher changed?

If the preacher doesn't reach and hold his congregation within the first half minute of the commencement of his sermon he has probably lost them as attentive listeners for that Sunday at least. An observant preacher can learn from the media. Popular journalism, as in the *Reader's Digest* and *Time* magazine, pays particular attention to the opening paragraphs. For example, here is the opening of an article on Martin Luther published in the October 1983 edition of *Time* magazine:

> It was a back-door deal, little different from many others struck at the time, but it triggered an upheaval that altered irrevocably the history of the western world.

Contrast that with the opening sentence of a typical Sunday sermon: 'In today's Gospel, my dear people, we see how Jesus went about doing good'. On many occasions the sermon is simply a paraphrase of the readings that have already been read at Mass. Much of today's media is highly professional and skilled, and it has something to teach those of us who seek to proclaim the Gospel.

The men and women of this generation are not necessarily better or worse than they were thirty years ago. But the filtering and interpreting mechanism through which messages pass has been conditioned by a variety of factors of which the communications explosion must be one of the most important. If the pastor is transmitting with an outdated cultural baggage and a vocabulary that is archaic and in a style that is grating, then few if any of the congregation will have the receiver tuned in to accept and appropriate the message. If the preacher feels his message is falling on deaf ears it may not be that people are resisting the Gospel but rather that the transmitter and receivers are tuned to different wavelengths. Bishop Cahal Daly of Ireland emphasised this point in a talk to the International Catholic Union of the Press in 1984: 'Media have created a new style, a new language in communication generally, and new expectations in audiences. Religious communication must adapt to these new conditions or else fail to communicate.'

I read somewhere that 85% of what we learn comes through our eyes. If this is true it poses a real challenge to the Sunday morning preacher who has to rely on the power of his own eloquence and, of course, the Holy Spirit! I know some priests have dabbled with the use of audio-visual aids in Church. No matter how effective these might be there is always an element of gimmickry about them that is more likely to repel than attract the average churchgoer. However there is a definite place for modern media in the classroom and in the small group situation.

In a recent survey of preaching conducted for the Irish Liturgical Commission the majority of those questioned were demanding that the preacher make the connection between the Gospel and the reality of their daily lives. They wanted to know the relevance of the Gospel to the lives they led. The grist of daily living will only be collected by the preacher if he listens. What is behind the smiling faces? What are the pains and achievements that most affect the lives of his people? What is the faith motivation, if any, that gets them to Mass on Sunday? What do death and separation and alcoholism and success mean? What is the challenge most likely to draw the best qualities from people? What do mothers think? How do fathers see their role? What are the pressures on the people we preach to every Sunday? The real challenge is to make the connection between the reality of daily living and the reality of the Gospel.

The good communicator is a perceptive person, with the senses open, and sensitive to every reality; a reflective person, not just asking how things are, but why they are as they are, not necessarily praising or blaming but only seeking to understand. The capacity to be reflective is stimulated by a critical analysis of what is perceived, observed.

Why is it that people who claim not to watch television are so self-righteous? Those who neglect the media altogether consider this to be a virtue! How can the preacher make the necessary connection between the ordinariness of life lived at the coal face and the reality of the Gospel if he neglects to have some knowledge of the world of media? The goings-on in Coronation Street and the gossip in the Rovers' Return, have a reality for many people that the Gospel is unlikely to have. The 'ups and downs' of the lives of Rita Fairclough, Bet Lynch and Ken Barlow are awaited with eager anticipation. The **Archers**, **East Enders**, **Glenroe** and **Dallas** have an importance in people's lives second only to family births, marriages and deaths. Even though the pastor has little love for 'the soaps' it is advantageous to view these programmes occasionally and note the style, language and values contained in them.

In the gospel according to Madison Avenue, what we buy defines who we are. The advertising viewed daily creates expectations that are largely unachievable, especially by the poor. It was claimed that exciting holiday advertising encouraged Dublin's so-called Bugsy Malone gang to rob to fund exotic holidays on the Costa del Sol. The only times that people are presented as uniformly happy and ecstatically fulfilled are in commercials: purchasing, collecting or consuming products that resolve problems, deliver self-assurance, win friends. As Joan Evans of the Evans Marketing Group in New York has said: 'Any industry that sells hope is going to continue to grow. And that's what we're selling'.

The commercials offer instant solutions to the drudgery of life. A pill for every ill is the advertiser's ersatz promise. Beaming housewives clean floors in seconds. Headaches disappear immediately. Mortgages, life assurance, waft away financial problems. Advertising proposes that we 'transform our lives by buying something more'. Nirvana is here!

Advertising is probably far less effective than it is reputed to be. Nevertheless it is very much part of consumer society and its existence cannot be ignored by the pastor.

A common fault of the preacher is to condemn all media and to attribute to them most of the ills of society. Churchpeople and politicians too give far more weight to a negative press than it deserves.

A religious bookshop was asked by the Church authorities to withdraw a book from circulation. The media got wind of the decision and made much of it. The message of withdrawal did not reach another shop in the group which continued to sell the publication, much to the delight of the media, who made it headline news in the local paper. Previously a survey indicated that most people in that city did not know the location of the shop. After the so-called exposé, everyone knew, much to the firm's advantage.

It is probably better to avoid direct condemnatory reference to the media in sermons and talks. Criticising the media doesn't often produce results. Much of the criticism that is received by television and radio stations is ill-informed. Most media criticism is extremely prejudiced and ill-intent can seldom be proved.

Alluding to particular programmes and media personalities can become mere parochialism and is readily seen as material of the 'hobby horse' variety. Using media illustrations well-known to the congregation is a different matter.

The effects of the present immersion in media can easily be overestimated. People are resilient and find ways of keeping a balance in their lives. Nevertheless their basic experience, images and perceptions are being shaped by media in an incalculable way. Their attention is 'displaced'. The danger here is that just as the industrial revolution in the nineteenth century led to a continuing division between the working classes and the Church, so the communications revolution of today could separate new masses of people from the outreach of the Gospel.

The unchanging Gospel must be communicated in symbols, models, images and words that are accessible to each culture and understood by it. We have to rediscover the image dimension of the Gospel. The extraordinary success of the book *Jonathan Livingston Seagull* demonstrates the power of story telling. The wide popularity of Tolkien's *Middle Earth*, of Lewis's *Narnia* series, of *Watership Down*, suggests that the modern mind is quite sophisticated about myth, and hungry for it. It would be dangerous to suggest that the communications age rejects story, allegory or fable to illustrate a point.

Having said all this, in the last analysis it is the preacher's faith and sincerity that will probably convert more people than slick presentation. Eyeball-to-eyeball contact is the way that Christianity is spread. Every form of Christian communication, no matter how worthwhile, is in some way defective because it attempts to communicate love at a distance and that is to turn the incarnation on its head. In addition, communication is an act of corporeal presence and it demands self-disclosure on the part of the person passing on the information. Without self-disclosure, there is no communication.

Chapter Five

Media Relations — Vatican Style

The Roman Catholic Church has always had a love/hate relationship with the media. Its basic stance has been one of ambivalence. But ambivalence is an advance on the initial attitude of hostility and condemnation adopted by Pope Gregory XVI when he was first confronted by the French liberal Catholics Lamennais, Lacordaire, and Montalembert, who were crusading for an alliance between Church and 'democratic freedom'. Lamennais believed that only in an atmosphere of freedom, where all beliefs were equally tolerated, where there was freedom of the press, where any group might educate children according to its own principles, would the Church regain her soul. Gregory regarded it as impious to say that the Church had lost her soul.

The Church found it very difficult to come to grips with the pluralist, mass-mediated culture that began to emerge at the beginning of the last century. The French Revolution, the rise of Napoleon and the arguments about freedom, spearheaded by the French triumvirate, were more than the Vatican could comfortably take, and Gregory let fly with the publication of the encyclical, *Mirari Vos*, in 1832. The Pope was undoubtedly angered by the paper, *L'Avenir* (the future), which propagated 'dangerous' ideas about freedom of the press, freedom of association and freedom of speech which are commonplace today. *Mirari Vos* did not mince words:

> Here belongs that vile and never sufficiently execrated and detestable freedom of the press for the diffusion of all sorts

of writings: a freedom which, with so much insistence, they dare to demand and promote. We are horrified, venerable brothers, contemplating what monstrosities of doctrine, or better, what monstrosities of error are everywhere disseminated in a great multitude of books, pamphlets, written documents — small certainly in their size but enormous in their malice — from which goes out over the face of the earth that curse we lament.

In July 1861 the Vatican established its own 'newspaper', *L'Osservatore Romano*. It has never been a newspaper in the accepted sense of reporting facts and opinions and probing the background to the news. It is a 'house journal', propagandist in tone and content. 'Compared with *L'Osservatore Romano, Pravda* positively bristles with gossip', the *Economist* once stated with some degree of truth. Pope Paul VI is claimed to have said of his own newspaper: 'it reports on meetings before they have actually met'. The vast bulk of *L'Osservatore Romano* is taken up with papal speeches and writings. Any features it carries are always written by carefully selected and vetted authors, always clerical, in my experience. It is an important medium in so far as it carries the Papal message to the universal Church in a number of different language editions.

The attitude of the Papacy to the rising tide of liberal thought and influence was concretised in the *Syllabus of Errors* published in 1864 by Pius IX. In relation to freedom of speech the Pope refused to recognise that it ought to be laid down as a principle of universal validity that there should be absolute freedom of speech and absolute freedom of the press.

The relationship between the Church and the secular media was at best indifferent, at worst hostile, up to and even during the Second Vatican Council. Gary MacEoin, a journalist with a lifetime of experience in dealing with bureaucracies writes wryly of his first encounter with Vatican media relations men on the occasion of the Council. (*Memoirs and Memories*, 23rd Publications, p. 157):

As a result of the outraged protests of journalists at the first session of the Council, the Vatican's information service had purportedly been modernised and streamlined. But the change was strictly cosmetic, and not much of that. Typewriters had been provided, almost all with Italian keyboards unusable by the rest of us accustomed to the keyboards standard elsewhere. Soap and toilet paper were almost invariably lacking in the toilets. When some of us protested, the problem was solved by locking the toilets. Whenever an interview or function worth attending was announced, one had to get a special pass. The *tessera*, it turned out, was mainly useful because without it one could not apply for the special pass.... Unlike press facilities at the meetings of international bodies with which we were familiar, this system was designed to conceal from us what was happening and make selective disclosure of such facts as its manipulators either judged would advance the Vatican's interests — as they conceived them — or such facts as could be sold by insiders for cash or for balancing favours.

Nevertheless, the Council marked a *volte face* of considerable proportions in the Church's attitude to the secular media. The conciliar decree, *Inter Mirifica*, dealing with the mass media, was generally considered to be substandard in comparison to other conciliar documents. However, it did state emphatically that 'the media are there for the good of everyone and to serve everyone'.

The document was important if only because it was the first time that the Church had given any concentrated thought to the mass media. It urged that priests, religious and lay people be trained in media techniques so that the Church would have the opportunity not only of contributing to the secular media on behalf of the Church but of using modern means of communication to further the promulgation of the Gospel.

Inter Mirifica authorised the holding of a World Communications Day. This would be an occasion for dialogue with media personnel and it was hoped that sermons in churches throughout the world would enable Catholics to become more conscious of the potential of the media. The Holy See, at the direction of *Inter Mirifica*, established what is now the Pontifical Commission for Social Communications. The decree also asked that 'national offices for the press, the cinema, radio and television be established everywhere and be properly supported'. In each country the working of these offices was to be overseen by an episcopal commission appointed by the national hierarchy.

The most significant milestone in the Church's attitude to the media was marked by the publication of the *Pastoral Instruction on the Means of Social Communication* in 1977. The prestigious Paris newspaper, *Le Monde*, described the document as 'presenting an information policy that reversed all the habits of governmental thought and practice within the Catholic Church.' Leading Vaticanologist Peter Hebblethwaite describes it as 'an explosive little document'. He wrote recently, 'This document had a very tonic effect in the developed world, where relations between the press and the bishops improved as the bishops acquired professional press officers and were educated into some understanding of the media' (*In the Vatican*, Oxford University Press, p. 184). Bishop Agnellus Andrew OFM, the late doyen of religious broadcasters, wrote in *The Tablet* that 'the new document is open and liberal and deals with the mass media in a way that is eminently modern and practical.'

Communio et Progressio (community and advancement) benefited greatly from the broad level of consultation that went into its drafting. The Pontifical Commission included among the consultors lay people professionally involved in the media. The hierarchies throughout the world were constantly consulted about the various drafts.

Communio et Progressio had the advantage of gaining from the insights of the recent Council. The opening tone of the Instruction is positive: 'The Church sees the media as "gifts from God" which, in accordance with his providential design, unite men in brotherhood and so help them to co-operate with his plan for salvation.'

The document is comprehensive. It is underpinned by a doctrinal foundation which details God's plan in salvation history. 'In the fullness of time, he communicated his very self to men and "the Word made flesh" ...communication among men found its highest ideal and supreme example in God who had become man and brother.'

The document is practical — it deals with the real world. Public opinion, the right to be informed, education, culture, leisure, training in the use of the media, opportunities and obligations are all dealt with, as are the specific media of radio, television, theatre and the press.

In *Communio et Progressio* there is an understanding of and sensitivity towards the difficulties inherent in the newsgathering task. There is a condemnation of violence directed against journalists. Even the editorial role of choosing what makes news is commented on 'out of a mass of material they must select what they judge to be the significant facts that will concern their audience. So it can happen that the news reported is only a part of the whole and does not convey what is of real importance' (par. 37). The danger of news distortion arising out of the quick comment is mentioned: 'Because the media are impelled to demand quick comment, the initiative often passes to men who are less responsible and less well-informed, but who are more willing to oblige'. The constraints of time under which the newsperson works and the cut-throat competition in the media business leads to mistakes. As the document points out, 'speed is often won at the price of accuracy'.

One pivotal passage in *Communio et Progressio* urges that: 'The liberality which is an essential attribute of the Church demands that the news she gives out be distinguished by integrity, truth and openness, and that these should cover her intention as well as her works'.

The important documents *Inter Mirifica* and *Communio et Progressio* have been followed up with expressions of good intent, many unfortunately unfulfilled. Archbishop Foley, the President of the Pontifical Commission on Social Communications, admitted as much. 'We at the Vatican must do much more to guarantee the speedy transmission of accurate and authentic information.' Speaking to Catholic journalists he said: 'If we do not take the initiative in transmitting accurate and authentic information about the Church, then who will? Do we have an adequate network of news services in the world?' (Talk to Catholic journalists, June 1985) Pope John Paul is reported to have said that the Church ought to be like a glasshouse, 'visible equally from within and without'.

Unfortunately, this statement must surely convict even the most zealous supporter of Vatican media relations. I have been present at the fringe of several synods and media relations are more frequently conducted in contradiction of *Communio et Progressio* and other Papal pronouncements than in conformity with them. For instance in a scholarly and informative book on the 1980 Synod of Bishops, *On the Role of the Family* (Leuven University Press, 1983), the following familiar criticism is made:

> Another aspect of this Synod in particular was the greater closedness surrounding its procedure than any of the earlier meetings. The direction given to the process and the division of labour were of such a nature that the bishops had very little contact among themselves and were practically cut off from the observers and from the outside world. During the most crucial phase, namely the task of working out the suggestions in the Propositions, there was not a single press release issued for five days. On several occasions, the fatal result was a one-sided image of the events presented in the media.

The publication of *Communio et Progressio* has failed to bring about a deep and lasting change in the relationship between Vatican congregations and personnel, and the professional media. It was distressing to see well-established journalists herded into a corral at the entrance to the Synod Hall during recent synods. From such a position they lack even the possibility of speaking to the bishops as they enter and leave. This type of ungenerous treatment generates justifiable anger against the Vatican. In November 1987 Sean Mac Réamoinn wrote in *Doctrine and Life* of the inadequacies of the Vatican media relations: 'Alas! the Vatican has not yet caught up with the idea of having a Press Gallery on such occasions. Indeed, its ancient mania for secrecy and its more recently acquired realisation that Communication is a Good Thing are still locked in a very odd kind of struggle, which produces very odd effects'. One of the most trenchant critics of Vatican media practice is Peter Hebblethwaite. He claims that 'the Vatican remains a secretive society, a closed shop'.

The apparent lack of openness in dealing with the Marcinkus

affair and the lack of any response to the accusations of David Yallop or Gordon Thomas leave the media consumer puzzled, to say the least.

On occasions the Vatican's own Press Office has been unaware of the release of important documents by other Vatican departments and is thus not in a position to supply background information or comment — both essential to the working journalist. Another difficulty is that Vatican documents are often released through the international press agencies and so are available throughout the world before local Church press offices have an opportunity of studying the material.

After the Vatican Council, a wave of euphoria washed over the Church. *Aggiornamento* was the word on everyone's lips. At the same time as the ecclesiastical renewal or updating, the explosion in communications technology was taking place. A television set was a novelty. Television itself didn't know what to do with religion. Men nattering in pubs over a pint of stout were confused and uncertain when confronted with Benediction of the Blessed Sacrament. Should they kneel down? Stop talking? Or irreverently ignore the sacred ceremony? Priests flocked to courses on effective communications. Now that media professionals have honed their skill to a fine art, some of the most important suggestions of *Communio et Progressio* have been forgotten. Seventeen years ago the Instruction stated:

> If students for the priesthood and religious in training wish to be part of modern life and also to be at all effective in the apostolate, they should know how the media work upon the fabric of society, and also the technique of their use. This knowledge should be an integral part of their ordinary education.

In my experience this is not happening. Even verbal communication (homiletics) is a low priority on the curriculum of most seminaries.

The Congregation for Catholic Education's *Guide to the Training of Future Priests Concerning the Instruments of Social Communication*, published in Rome in 1986, stated that effective and organic programmes were still almost totally lacking, either because the specific object and scope of any programme was poorly understood, or because there had been a failure to distinguish between aims and levels which had been visualised in the proposal. Another difficulty was that staff qualified to prepare and carry out training programmes in communications were in short supply. There was also an absence of technical and economic resources.

John Paul II has addressed the subject of media on many occasions. It is obvious that he recognises the potential and power of the media. Addressing the Bishops of Provence-Mediterranée, he said, 'Yes, the means of social communication in today's world are very powerful and omnipresent, and their influence will undoubtedly become even greater.' He is also convinced of the responsibilities of and the possibilities available to the good journalist. In a talk to journalists on 27 January 1984 he said: 'Your mission can illuminate, or orientate and sustain everything which really helps authentic and integral progress in human society. It can open up horizons to minds and hearts. It can stimulate individuals towards those objectives which work in favour of a better quality of life. In a word, it can arouse and stimulate all those yeasts upon which the salvation of mankind depend in the agitated and promising present period.' He urged the journalists to be tuned in to 'the waves of reality'. The following year, addressing the International Catholic Union of the Press, he praised the function of contemporary journalism, saying it 'often seeks out the hidden sinners of society, so that their crimes may be revealed and so that society may be healed. This service can indeed be salutary'.

In an address to the International Catholic Union of the Press in 1981, he said: 'It is the duty for Christian communities in the dioceses, as on the national and international planes, to pursue and intensify their effort to promote the Church's own information media, so that news about the internal life of the Church and her activities, as well as the word and the teachings of the successors of the apostles, may be transmitted freely and with a concern for accuracy'.

The Latin American Bishops' meeting in Puebla concluded a long statement on the mass media by stressing that 'knowing the situation of poverty, marginalisation and injustice in which large masses of Latin Americans are immersed, and also being aware of the violation of human rights, in its use of its own media the Church must more and more each day become the voice of the dispossessed, even at the risk entailed'.

A working paper submitted to the federation of Asian Bishops' Conferences in 1982 charts the evolution of the relationship between Church and media.

The first attitude, that adopted by Pope Gregory was one of suspicion and rejection. If the media is seen only as a danger then the only logical practical action is one of protection through censorship. The Church declared some books, films and theatre sinful or leading to sin. Up to the time of the Vatican Council priests were strictly forbidden to attend any theatrical performances!

As the world began to change and it was no longer possible to forbid under pain of sin, a new attitude of 'Why should the devil have all the best tunes?' emerged. In other words, 'Let's beat them at their own game'. Many local churches felt compelled to combat the influence of the media with a media of their own. Paul Crouch, one of America's now discredited tele-evangelists, put it this way:

> High in the midst of heaven a drama so immense is taking place that Satan and all of hell is reeling from the impact. The Prince of the Power of the Air is no longer the undisputed Prince. A new invasion beach-head has been launched into the airwaves! Praise the Lord. ANGEL II is in orbit; that tiny-winged piece of electronic miracle is picking up 'let's Praise the Lord'. Twenty-four hours a day Christian television is now raining down on half the Western hemisphere'. (Paul Crouch, as quoted by Peter Elvy, *Buying Time*, McCrimmon Publishing, p. 19).

More and more Church communicators are willing to work alongside their lay professional peers. The idea of religious broadcasting on an exclusive channel certainly finds little favour among clerical personnel involved in media. More and more they see their task as being to work alongside the existing media; to fight their corner but be part of that media. The response of the English hierarchy to the government's Green Paper was to reject the proposal that broadcasting channels might be farmed out to religious groups and churches. And so, in the third trend, the Church began to look at the media from the inside. The idea of service finds an application in the mass media, for the communications media constitute one of the main forms of contemporary social life. A study of media and an appreciation of the difficulties and possibilities led to a critical understanding, discriminatory use and compassionate service. *Communio et Progressio*, speaking of Church communicators, states: 'They are not at this work in order to dominate the media with their viewpoint but, rather, they aim to give a service.'

Evolution of the Relationship between Church and Media

	Attitude	Action	Position
Trend One	Suspicion and Rejection	Censorship and Control	Outside
Trend Two	Irritation and Ambition	Use at any Cost	Marginal
Trend Three	Critical Understanding	Discriminatory Use and Compassionate Service	Inside

WACC, 122 Kings Road, London SW3 4TR (from *Media Development*, Vol XXXI, 1984).

Part Two

Practice, not Theory

Introduction

I am a generalist rather than a specialist. The generalist flounders in the world of communications. Most of what he says is an informed guess. How much does violence in the media influence human behaviour? Is media advertising effective? What is the relationship between media and culture? The specialist researcher, the academic, spends long hours investigating such questions. Who would ever have thought it possible to gain a university degree in communications twenty-five years ago? In reserching the material for this book I was overwhelmed by the sheer volume of technical and academic writing available on the theory of communications. The theorising and theologising on the communications revolution is endless. Gnarled veterans of the media world began as messenger boys or tea-makers. Not any more. Now a university degree or its equivalent is necessary. The most damning comment of an episcopal gentleman of my acquaintance about a fellow cleric was, 'the fellow knows no theology'. In the specialist world of media a similar comment is frequently made. Today's specialists guard their 'turf' with a disdain for the general practitioner. I am not writing this in a critical spirit. The critical questions are not ones of technique. The real question is: 'What is it all for?' But, meanwhile, the band plays on. Programmes are produced. The voracious appetite of the media for material is insatiable. Ordinary mortals must face the muzzles of microphone or camera and that is why the second part of this book is being written.

Many people allow themselves to be intimidated by the media. 'No comment' is safe. And yet mass media, no matter how bad it is, provides an invaluable service to the wider community. It is better to be in the thick of it rather than criticising from the sidelines.

Some people stumble into television notoriety, like Paul Nolan, an unemployed window cleaner from Bournemouth who found stardom after a single appearance on a popular television show. Others, such as politicans and trades union leaders have it thrust upon them. For the majority, even popular media presenters, it is hard work, some talent, preparation, and being in the right place at the right time. There is another group which needs the media to massage their egos, the 'instant comment' merchants, who have a press statement for every spoken thought. Invariably this latter group unconsciously exposes its own superficiality mercilessly.

You may recall that *Communio et Progressio* urged Church personnel to become involved in media work. It said:

> As representatives of the Church, bishops, priests, religious, and laity are increasingly asked to write in the press, or appear on radio and television, or to collaborate in filming. They are warmly urged to undertake this work.

The document stresses that the complexity of the media requires a sound knowledge of the impact of the media and the best way of using them. It emphasises the importance of making certain 'that those who have to use the media receive sufficient and timely training'.

Obviously the best training is 'hands-on' experience. A formal training course is always helpful. It is not always possible to avail of either of these options. It is for these reasons that the second portion of this book sets out to give some general help to those who are asked to use the media infrequently. It is for those who have no ambition to be 'stars' but who recognise the importance of grasping every available opportunity to reach far more people than the Sunday sermon could ever hope to capture.

If this section prevented a blasé and 'couldn't-care-less' approach to the media it will have gone a long way towards accomplishing what it set out to do. Just as we wouldn't drive a car, deliver a lecture, undertake a long journey, without preparation, we have to respect the modern means of communications and the professional media people, many of whom are professionals to their fingertips.

Chapter One

Radio

RADIO IS STILL ALIVE AND WELL

In a limited survey I conducted among final year secondary school pupils the results indicated that these young people depended on television and, to a lesser extent, on newspapers to obtain news and information. For them television was a more authoritative medium. Radio was for music. Despite this there are indications that radio is on the way back. A radio is standard equipment in any new car. The small compact transistor is invariably a travelling companion. Bedtime is radio time.

As I write this the Irish Parliament is considering a bill to establish a new national independent radio station, twenty-six country-wide stations, up to 100 town stations with a radius of 8-10 miles and up to 100 neighbourhood stations with a radius of 2-5 miles. The British Home Secretary also proposes to introduce a bill in Parliament in Autumn 1988 which will authorise the creation of three national commercial radio stations and several hundred local and community stations. So radio is back in a big way.

Radio as a medium has an immediacy that television lacks. When news of the horrific Ethiopian famine broke I had the opportunity of joining some media people on the first mercy flight out of Ireland. On my return I was able to phone the radio station from the airport to give them a resumé of my experience, drive to the station and be interviewed for the next news programme. Television would have demanded much more planning.

The phone-in means that the person in the street has the

opportunity of expressing a view on air. The ease with which an outside broadcast can be arranged gives radio a versatility that television usually lacks.

Radio affords more opportunity to the ordinary person to obtain airtime. It has an insatiable appetite for news material. Programmers have a lot of time to fill. Interviewees fail to turn up. An interview finishes short of its allotted time. If you think you have an interesting story my advice is — try radio first.

RADIO

A television studio is an intimidating place for the uninitiated. Blazing lights, neck or clip-on microphones, cables littering the floor, the need for make-up, people with clipboards, all combine to unsettle all but the gnarled veteran. Before a television programme, even the interviewer can appear nervous. The television camera is a prying, exposing, inquisitive instrument. Like the boxing ring, once the programme begins, there's nowhere to run for refuge.

Radio is a much friendlier medium. It's more intimate, more personal. Television didn't signal the doom of radio as some predicted. In the United States there are nearly 9,000 radio stations, of which 1,400 are religious radio stations. In Britain alone there are some forty local radio stations. There are 850 million radio sets in the world. During a cab ride from the airport in Boston recently, a religious radio programme played continuously. When we arrived at my destination, I asked the driver 'Were you trying to convert me?' He laughed and said, 'Man, I wouldn't miss that preacher every day for any fare!' I don't think he was unique. The transistor and the car radio mean that the airwaves are accessible to most people worldwide. As I write this, **Morning Ireland**, Ireland's most popular early morning radio news programme is conducting an interview with an Irish government minister from the car telephone as he journeys from Limerick to Dublin.

The Irish Parliament recommended that from its inception 'broadcasting should be a state service purely — the installation and the working of it to be solely in the hands of the Postal Ministry'. The subsequent Act of 1926 provided for the establishment and maintenance of state broadcasting stations. Obviously, this means that it is difficult for local community and vocational groups to have any access to the airwaves, except to receive existing programmes. All broadcasting is at the behest of the personnel of the existing state service. The establishment of local or community radio has been delayed, apparently because of wrangling at political level.

Radio is an intimate medium. Watching television is an activity for which you have to set time aside. You can drive a car, clean a house, sunbathe or garden while listening to the radio.

Radio has far more of the element of the one-to-one than television, which partakes more of the show-biz dimension of life. The **Morning Ireland** programme in the background is a series of one-to-one interviews, with two presenters providing the linking snippets.

THE RADIO INTERVIEW

Because the radio is more of a one-to-one medium, it ought to be conducted in your natural conversational tone of voice. The humour, modulation, pitch and tone of normal conversation is right for radio. People want to hear a man or woman 'talking'. From the voice and the subject material, the listener paints the picture and provides the images that will hold the interest and keep the listener tuned in. Is it because the pulpit preacher sounds so resonantly artificial that people tend to switch off?

Preparation is just as important for radio as for television. Never forget that the interviewer has the assistance of researchers and a producer to provide basic information and suggest the line of questioning to be adopted. It is possible for notes to be used on radio, whereas on television they are a distraction. I can recall being on a radio chat show with a Baptist minister on one occasion. He used notes copiously and skillfully. His conversational tone of voice never changed. I know that on that occasion I sounded particularly ignorant in comparison. Most trainers will caution against the use of notes. I believe that if you have your material well prepared and you are familiar with your subject, then good 'prompter' notes or cards can be an asset.

If you have to wade through a sheaf of notes to find what you want, with all the attendant rustling and fuss, then it would be better to have left them at home.

A radio studio is simpler than its television counterpart. All the gadgets are behind soundproof glass. A table with a microphone in front of you, facing the interviewer, is not that intimidating! A voice test will be taken — this may happen during the commercial break if the interview is live and part of an ongoing programme. Speak into the microphone and continue to use the same tone and volume.

In many ways, radio is more difficult than television. On the television the interviewer is unlikely to let you 'dry up' completely. The medium is more demanding of continuous action. Radio is a conversation. Therefore, a series of monosyllabic answers will make for boring radio and certainly will not do your case any good. Your answers should supply colour and background, interlaced with very brief anecdotes or stories. In general, as long as you keep up an interesting, stimulating flow of talk, the interviewer will not interrupt.

Beware of the manipulative interviewer. The questions they ask are really disguised statements. The manipulative interviewer asks a question in such a way that the other person has no option but to agree or disagree with him. 'Do you think that . . . .?'

The 'star' interviewers suffer from the disease of narcissism. They want to draw attention to themselves. They end up speaking more than the interviewee. They will make comments like 'Very good', 'What you say is very interesting', 'Exactly'. They adopt a paternalistic or falsely congenial tone. They feel superior and let you know it. If you are well prepared and know your subject, don't allow yourself to be diverted by this treatment. You have something to say — say it.

Let the interviewer be your audience. You are talking to one person. If you do that well, you will keep the interest of many. So focus your attention on that person. It is important to remember that most people who listen to the radio do so alone.

Delivery is more important on radio than on television. On the television your facial expression, gesture and tone of voice all signal messages to the viewer. Not so on radio. A radio interview is more of an intimate conversation, and you can, therefore, interrupt to assist the interviewer.

Obviously, the tone of voice is important. You need to sound sincere and enthusiastic. Your body language can flow over into your voice. Voice reveals how you really feel. Don't be bullied or baited. In particular, don't allow yourself to become aggressive.

Radio demands quick thinking. You must prepare and be alert. Listen attentively to the questions you are asked, but at the same time if you have a definite point you wish to make, do so under one of the question heads. Try to answer the questions if you can. How often have you been a frustrated listener as politicians duck and wave to avoid the interviewer's questions?

Chapter Two

Newspapers

Enough news arrives daily at any large newspaper office to make four or five novels and fill the news column many times over. The *New York Times* receives 2,000,000 words on an average day. It publishes 185,000.

The raw material for news can come from anywhere. The 'cat stranded up a tree' story can be phoned in to a newspaper office by the owner, the rescuer, a gardener. In 1979, animal lovers jammed the switchboard at ITN to complain about a news item concerning a cat. The story had been read by newsreader Reginald Bosanquet, who ended the *News at Ten* with a report about an emergency call that had been received from an old lady.

Reporters undertake daily chores, phoning the fire brigade, the local police station, the contact at the ambulance service — in search of news. They attend court hearings, meet VIPs, attend press conferences, council meetings, political party events, coroner's inquests, sporting events, 'high society' jamborees, pop concerts — the list is endless.

Most large daily newspapers will have a stable of special correspondents who are constantly generating stories in their own special fields; be it agriculture, diplomacy, religion, the arts or whatever.

The international news agencies, like Reuter, UPI (United Press International) and others, supply subscribing media with daily news. For instance, in Britain, PA (the Press Association) provides a constant stream of news stories on a telex machine to each provincial newspaper as well as the national newspapers in Britain and Ireland and the broadcasting newsrooms in

London. Two hundred and fifty journalists work a twenty-four hour shift, seven days a week, to produce a daily total of 220,000 words.

As if that isn't enough, newspaper offices are inundated with press releases, publicity material, scripts and feature material, both commissioned and unsolicited.

Media professionals are inherently cannibalistic — they poach stories from each other. The lead stories in the morning papers will most likely become fodder for chat shows later in the day. Stories in one paper will be investigated in greater detail by another.

So, if you want to get into the news, you have got to have something worth saying. Not as easy as it might seem. Over the years, the regular suppliers of news have learned how to use the media for their own benefit. Name the six most prominent public figures whose voices or images are heard or seen with monotonous regularity in Ireland. I have a hunch that in this country two politicians of the 'left', one senior Church of Ireland clergyman, one Catholic bishop, the editor of a daily newspaper, and an official of a leading farmers' organisation would be included in most people's list. Why? These people are often in a position to use the carrot and the stick technique with the media. It is never said openly, but if the media refuse to play ball, then information will be witheld, 'off the record' briefings will be denied. For instance, reporters who are regularly critical of the police can land themselves in trouble. According to Brian Whittaker in *News Ltd*, Thomas Bryant, a freelance reporter, faced forty-seven charges, including dishonest handling of the *Police Gazette* and confidential police information and photographs, and inciting an officer to commit a breach of discipline. The charges were eventually dismissed. Bryant believed that he was hounded because he had 'never been afraid to write stories which have often upset the police'. Simon Hoggart of the *Guardian* tells similar stories about the relationship between the army and the media in Northern Ireland. 'Tell it as we say it is, or you will be frozen out of all news sources.'

Simon Winchester, also a *Guardian* reporter, describes a typical Northern Ireland situation. 'The gunfire that began around 8.30

p.m. went on and on and it invited the inevitable reply by the army. To anyone who experienced the battle it was perfectly obvious that hundreds and hundreds of bullets were being fired by both sides, and yet the army had the gall, when asked by reporters later in the weekend, to say that its soldiers had fired only fifteen shots in sum.' The official figures were to be published later. Soldiers in the Falls that weekend fired no less than 1,457 bullets.

Even since those later figures were quietly published, many reporters found it very hard to accept contemporary accounts from the army public relations personnel.

Special interest groups like political parties, trades unions, large, established Churches and vocational bodies, have the resources to employ press officers or public relations personnel. These are usually former journalists with the inside track on the techniques of promoting their personality or brand or image. Large companies budget resources for public relations. Malcolm Muggeride has described PR as 'organised lying'.

According to Tom Baistow in *Fourth Rate Estate:* 'Everyone from the Prime Minister to the latest rock star and, not least, big business, has something they want to sell, from ideas and personal images to consumer goods and services; it is an equation that the public relations industry has cashed in on at various levels. The unsuspecting reader is unlikely to have noticed it, but to the practised eye more and more of both news and feature pages bear the often well-disguised print of the PR hand, from the 'Beauty Queen Drama' splash and picture filling page one to the middle-spread interview with Mrs Thatcher and the enthusiastic welcome in the City pages for the latest privatisation flotation.' He goes on to claim that 'the 110 member firms of the Public Relations Consultation's Association in Britain have a total income of 25 million a year, wth a total expenditure of some £500 million that indicates the ramifications of the all-pervasive PR network'.

In addition, establishment bodies have the resources to 'wine and dine' the press in lavish fashion. A recent letter to a Dublin newspaper claimed that the property page ought to be firmly designated as an advertising feature and not continue to masquerade as 'news'. Could the same apply to the motoring page and to the travel section? Can news be bought at the price of 'perks'?

It is difficult for the individual or for the small, weak organisation to make news. Occasionally, they will do so as figures of fun, like the Cork Councillor, Barney Murphy, who got himself invited to San Francisco for the St Patrick's Day festivities, or as unusual, as in the case of 'streakers'.

WHAT IS NEWS FOR THE PRESS?

When asked what news is, journalists usually reply, 'News is what you find in newspapers', 'News is what fills the space left by the adverts', or 'News is what somebody doesn't want you to know'.

According to Harold Evans, a former editor of the *Sunday Times*, 'News is people. It is people talking and people doing. Committees and cabinets and courts are people; so are fires, accidents and planning decisions. They are only news because they involve and affect people' (*The Practice of Journalism*, Hernemann, 1963). The meaning of news varies from country to country. While disasters and crimes and conflict and government make news in the West, in Russia it is the latest five-year plan or the Ukrainian grain harvest. And the biggest news story in Peking one morning was the discovery of a new way to prove that Pythagoras got his theorem right.

Stalin wrote 'The press is the strongest instrument with which day by day, hour by hour, the party speaks to the masses in their own essential language. There is no other means as flexible for establishing spiritual links between the party and the working class' (Anthony Buzek, *How the Communist Press Works*, Pall Mall Press, 1964).

Evans' definition seems closest to the truth. Notice how even national issues will be concretised in real people in order to simplify the story for the reader. So if a new income tax is the issue of the day — the newspapers will tell you how this affects Joe and Mary Bloggs who live in a semi on the Elms Estate. When the Herald of Free Enterprise capsised it was the human interest angle that always made the news — whether rescuers, victims or the rescued.

Essentially, news is treated by the newspaper as a crop which is harvested by reporters and then passes through a series of processors until a small quantity eventually reaches you, the consumer, as 'news'. So the reporters marked for daily assignment harvest the news. They work to a news editor who, in turn, reports to senior news executives. Editorial conferences are held at set intervals throughout the day when news developments are assessed and the priority to be given to each story is decided. In the final news selection process, chief sub-editors exercise an important influence. Feature writers will gather material on running stories for more comprehensive treatment or carry out investigative work where the facts of a situation warrant exposure in the public interest. Newspaper headlines frequently bear little relationship to the stories they headline. This angers people, but it is well to remember that a headline is not an act of journalism, it is an act of marketing.

Leader writers have the job of commenting editorially on the main issues of the day. The structuring of a newspaper is a team effort. 'The workings of a great newspaper', said Lord Cooper, feeling at last thoroughly rotarian, 'are of a complexity which the public seldom appreciates. The citizen little realises the vast machinery put into motion for him in exchange for his morning penny' (*Scoop*, Evelyn Waugh).

Despite the refining process, there is a certain capriciousness about news coverage. The radio critic of the London *Times*, David Wad,e has referred to what he calls the Great Communications Delusion:

> A topic has to reach a certain pretty intense level of excitement before it qualifies in the minds of newsmen for much attention. South Africa, for instance, seems to be in a state of permanent qualification, while any tyrannies practised by black African governments on their own people rarey seem to qualify at all. Starving Ethiopians rapidly become a media event while four million or so Afghan refugees do not. Somehow the non-qualifiers, no matter how deserving of attention, lack an element of drama.

Both Desmond Fennell in his book, *Beyond Nationalism* (Ward River Press, 1985), and Bishop Cahal Daly, in a speech to the International Catholic Union of the Press, make somewhat the same point. Bishop Daly says:

> One must question whether we are witnessing the emergence of a new media orthodoxy, which is as unquestioning and as unchallenged as in earlier times Christian or Catholic orthodoxy was unquestioning and unchallenged. Religious dogmatism is faith seeking understanding. Dogmatism is religion which no longer seeks understanding or genuine dialogue, but seeks to impose conformity. There is a danger that society may pass, almost without knowing it, from religious dogma to liberal-secularist dogmatism. Like any dogmatism, this must be challenged and resisted. It is good to question the unreflecting assumptions of a religious culture. But who will question the unreflecting assumptions of a liberal-secularist culture? Who will question the questioners?

Arnold Wesker, quoted in *Discrimination and Popular Culture* (Pelican Original, 1964), makes a blistering attack on the press. He claims 'It is the age of the big insult — trivia pays larger dividends, therefore, trivia must be what is wanted. Is this a deliberate policy to keep the nation cretinised by trivialities or does it stem from profound belief that the people of this country [England] are cretins from the start?'

Harold Evans, in *Editing and Design*, gives the following example of good editing. Version A is the story as it appeared in print. Version B is how the same report could have been written by quickly editing it on copy without deleting essential facts. Version C is how the story could have been rewritten, given fifteen minutes more than the time available for straight editing on copy. Try your hand by editing the original story without reading version B. Then rewrite the story completely and compare your attempt with version C.

Version A

ROAD TOLL STARTS CLIMB
by the Association Press

The toll of traffic deaths among Americans celebrating the nation's freedom rose steadily yesterday.

The count climbed to 110 for the Independence Day holiday period that began at 6 p.m. Wednesday and will end at midnight Sunday.

The National Safety Council commented that, while the number was pushing up, it was not keeping pace with the total for the corresponding time of the four-day Fourth of July observance in 1961 when it reached a record 509.

The worst single accident cost the lives of six members of a family from Butler, Pa., who had set out for a pleasure ride in their new car.

Dry, pleasant weather in most sections of the country encouraged heavy travel.

The council has estimated that motor vehicle accidents may kill 550 to 650 persons during the four-day Independence observance.

That would be a record far exceeding the hold mark for a July 4th period of 509 set in 1961.

The record for a holiday period of any kind was established during a four-day observance of Christmas in 1956. It is 706.

To draw comparisons, the Associated Press made a survey of traffic fatalities during the four-day non-holiday period running from 6 p.m. Wednesday, June 19, to midnight Sunday, June 23. The tally was 458.

Traffic deaths, holding at record levels, have averaged 100 a day through the first five months of this year.

July 4 boating accidents cost 12 lives and drownings 40.

Verson B

Traffic deaths among Americans celebrating the nation's freedom rose steadily yesterday.

The total is 110 for the Independence Day holidays that began at 6 p.m. Wednesday and will end at midnight Sunday. But, the National Safety Council says this is lower than the corresponding time in 1961 when a record 509 died.

The worst single accident yesterday killed six of a family from Butler, Pa. who had set out for pleasure in their new car.

Dry, pleasant weather in most parts encouraged heavy travel.

The council has estimated that car accidents may kill 550 to 650 this four-day holiday. That would be a record well over the old one of 509 in 1961.

The record for any holiday is 706 killed over four days at Christmas 1956.

For comparison, the Associated Press surveyed traffic deaths over the four-day non-holiday period from 6 p.m. Wednesday, June 19, to midnight Sunday, June 23. The tally was 458.

Traffic deaths, holding at record levels, have averaged 100 a day in the first five months of this year.

July 4 boating accidents cost 12 lives and drownings 40.

Version C

FAMILY OF SIX DIES
Road Toll at 110

(AP) Six of a family from Butler, Pa., out for pleasure in their new car, died yesterday in the worst accident so far of the Independence Day holidays.

The toll among Americans celebrating the nation's freedom rose steadily as dry pleasant weather encouraged heavy travel in most parts. By last night 110 had died since 6 p.m. on Wednesday.

The National Safety Council said, however, deaths were not keeping pace with last year. It had previously estimated that 550 to 650 might die between Wednesday and the end of the holiday on Sunday, which would top the Independence record of 509 deaths in 1961. The all-time record for holiday deaths is 706 over four days at Christmas, 1956.

PERSONNEL FUNCTIONS IN A NEWSPAPER

News Editor

The person who decides what makes news on any particular day is the news editor. The news editor will decide what stories are to be covered on any particular day, and may also choose the angle from which the story will be handled and which reporter is to be assigned to the story.

Copy Taster

On some of the largest newspapers, a copy taster will work to the news editor. The copy taster will look at news from outside sources and decide what is to be used and what will be rejected. When an item of news is rejected it is 'spiked'. The offending copy is impaled on a metal spike set in a wooden base. Once a piece of news is 'spiked' it is dead as far as coverage is concerned.

Editor

Ultimately, the single most important arbiter of what gets into a paper or a television news bulletin is the editor. The editor is central in laying down the overall news approach of the paper. This function is mainly exercised at a conference held each morning where all the department heads — news editor, features editor, women's page editor, sports editor — discuss the possible composition of the newspaper. Later in the day there will be other conferences where final decisions will be taken. If the editor thinks a story is important, then it will appear in the paper. Therefore, getting the editor on your side is probably the single most important step towards having your story covered.

In Ireland, there are ten national daily newspapers. Some, like the Northern Ireland based *Belfast Telegraph* and the *Newsletter* and *Irish News*, and the southern based *Cork Examiner*, have only a limited national circulation. These daily newspapers have a combined circulation of over a million. In addition, the English newspapers, in particular the tabloid or yellow press, are making significant inroads into the circulation of locally based papers.

The circulation figures for English newspapers in Ireland are as follows:

SUNDAY as at 28 June 1987

News of the World	172,050
People	82,500
Telegraph	7,500
Express	27,150
Mirror	70,025
Times	21,020
Observer	12,500
Mail	22,725

DAILY as at 1 July 1987

Mirror	82,125
Star	48,150
Express	8,500
Mail	4,700
Sun	25,600
Times	1,450
Today	3,025

The circulation figures for Irish newspapers are as follows:

DAILY January/June 1987

Irish Press	79,235
Irish Independent	151,150
Irish Times	88,739
Cork Examiner	58,509
Evening Press	125,291
Evening Herald	110,015
Evening Echo (Cork)	33,582
Belfast Telegraph	147,470

SUNDAY January/June 1987

Sunday Press	257,461
Sunday Independent	222,361
Sunday World	336,806
Sunday Tribune	96,660

It is interesting to note that the combined sales of the top three English newspapers (all tabloid), outstrip the sales of the largest selling Irish based newspapers. Over 155,000 Irish people depend on the English tabloids for their daily newspaper. The so-called quality newspapers cannot compete with their scruffier counterparts.

WRITING A PRESS RELEASE

The press release is the most usual way of communicating with the media. Large companies, politicial parties and trades union, all employ professionals, either in house or through a public relations company, to deal with the media on their behalf. A significant part of their job will be the writing of press releases. Every day, provincial and national newspapers receive dozens of press releases. A good press release on a topical and interesting subject can even find its way unedited into a newspaper. News editors and journalists like getting press releases — they save work.

A press release can give notice of a forthcoming event. It can carry a report of a meeting. Give punchy details of a speech — with complete script enclosed. It can provide an important statement, correction or clarification on a matter of important public interest.

Arrest attention with a good heading

It is a well-written headline that sells a story. A good headline will grab the reporter's or sub-editor's attention. Headlines are advertising. However, there is no need to be slick or to try to do the sub's work.

Use the active voice — 'Bishop opens new church' is preferable to 'New church opened by Bishop'.

Use the present tense — 'Choir beats Guinness record' rather than 'Choir beat Guinness record'.

Use short words where possible — 'Church repairs start' rather than 'Planned reconstruction on local church commences'.

One sentence — 'Picnic best ever' rather than 'Record attendance at best ever parish picnic'.

Put all your facts in the opening paragraph
A press release answers as briefly as possible the five w's — Who? What? Where? When? Why? Every press release should begin with the first four w's — What is happening? Who is doing it? Where it is happening? When it is happening?

Who?	Bishop Arthur Forbes
What?	will maracycle to Cork
Where?	commencing from the GPO Dublin
When?	next Thursday at 8.00 pm

Who?	The National Conference of Priests
What?	have appointed Fr Joe Bloggs as their new Chairman
When?	to take office immediately
Where?	at their Dublin headquarters.

The fifth w — Why? — explains the why of the other four w's. Take the two introductions above. The why follows naturally in each case: 'to raise funds for the Third World Mission in Kitui', or 'Fr Bloggs fills the vacancy created by the recent death of Fr Bill Howard in a road accident'.

Once you have got the basic facts out of the way, you can continue with the story.

Keep it short
The press release will tell the story as interestingly as possible. If it is an invitation to a press conference or to the launch of a product, giving every detail will discourage the paper from sending a reporter.

Use a quote if possible
Harold Evans said that news is about people — people doing and people talking. Every press release should include a quote. Sub-editors like quotes. They put a human face on an event.

Try to get a direct quote into the early part of the press release. If the Church is accused of neglecting the marginalised, a vigorous quote refuting the allegation will make news.

Bishop Joseph Hobbs rejected the allegation that the Church neglected the deprived. 'It is an absurd allegation', said Bishop Hobbs this morning. The Bishop, who was opening a new home for old folk at Northwinds Terrace, Dublin, claimed that 'over one quarter of the diocesan budget this year will go towards the care of the needy'.

Joe Black, the President of the St Martha's Benevolent Society, launched a national appeal for funds today at the Society's headquarters in Cork. 'It is not good enough that two out of the three people in this country haven't enough to eat', said Mr Black. 'I am appealing to the well-heeled in the community to give full support to our national church gate collection which will be taken up on the first Sunday of next month.'

Mr Black thanked the generosity of the Irish people who had contributed £2 million to last year's collection. 'This represents an extraordinary witness to the generosity of the Irish people'. Mr Black stated that the very severe winter had forced the Society to seek additional grants from the Government.

Give the name and telephone number of a contact person for further details

If your press release has managed to attract attention, a reporter will invariably be assigned to ferret out some further details. Give the name of a contact person, telephone number and the time the contact person is likely to be available.

If the press release is an invitation to a press reception, check to make sure the event is in the diary

All newspapers carry a daily diary of events to be covered by reporters or photographers. If you are not in the diary, then don't be disappointed if no one turns up. Check the day beforehand to see if your event is to be covered. Sometimes you may be neglected by oversight. A phone call might do the trick.

The embargo

An embargo means that you can send news to the media in advance of when you want it to appear. The timing of the embargo needs careful thought. Do you wish to make the morning or evening papers? If you embargo a press release until 12 noon, you may be early enough to make the evening nationals and it is unlikely that the following day's daily papers will be interested. There is always a running feud between the broadcasting and print media. If you embargo a press release, try to be fair to both. A late evening embargo may make the evening bulletin, thereby reducing the possibility of good coverage in the morning papers.

In general, embargoes are respected. Journalists have more to lose than to gain by breaking an embargo.

How your press release will look
Use headed notepaper.
Type your press release using double spacing.
Put the word 'Embargo' at the head of the release.
Type on one side of the paper.
Put a simple heading on the release.
If the press release contains more than one page, put the word 'more' indicating that there is more to come.
Number the pages.
Be sure to include the name, telephone number and availability of the contact person.
If you are releasing a speech or a very long statement, make a very short resumé, giving a number of the central points and the details of Who? What? Where? and When? Attach a copy of the full speech.

HOW TO ORGANISE A PRESS CONFERENCE
Organising a successful news conference depends very much on: the **importance** of the story you have to tell; the pressure of other, more newsworthy events on the same day; the suitability of the location and time, and the availability of reporters and photographers.

Holding a news conference is an invitation to **all** the media to come and meet you. It gives you the opportunity to talk personally to journalists and, more importantly, they are given an opportunity to ask searching questions.

Arranging a press conference entails time and money. An invitation to a press conference will not guarantee that the press will attend. An out-of-the-way location or an awkward time will demand that what you have to offer in the way of copy or pictures is important. There should always be a good story from a journalist's point of view. Remember, news is people, it is the unusual, the out-of-the-way — 'dog bites man is not news; man bites dog is'!

The first decision is whether or not to hold a press conference. The announcement of the springtime ball to raise funds for the local church may only be news if some important personality will be present, or if there will be possibilities for the photographers. Recently, I noticed complaints from a group of disabled athletes who had competed in a major international competition, won several medals and received little publicity. Even the Taoiseach has been known to complain when the national television neglected to send a camera crew to cover a function at which he was officiating. Even highly paid PR people sometimes fail to attract the media to their news conferences.

You have decided to hold a news conference on the occasion of the annual meeting and report of the diocesan social services. You begin by composing your invitation along the lines of the press release. Remember the five w's?

Where will the press conference be? When will it take place? What is it about? Who will be speaking? Why is it being held? You can give a few of the main points of what will be said. It may happen that some newspaper will be unavoidably absent, but would like to know of the event. Some reporters will ring and try to wrestle the complete story from you over the phone and so avoid attending. Either way, make sure the complete story is available immediately after the event and left into the offices of the newspapers or TV station.

For a Church-based press conference, lavish refreshments are not expected. A cup of tea and sandwiches are always welcome, or a glass of wine.

The press conference should be held in a suitable room with sufficient chairs. Even if all the national papers and the local TV station send representatives, the number attending will be small. It is not necessary to have an entourage of 'hangers on' present.

Have the basic facts available in printed form. For an annual report of the diocesan social services, state how much money you collected and disbursed. What are the major needs in the community and what plans have you to cope with them? Do you have a comment to make about local or central government funding?

Name the principle speaker(s) and their position(s) in the organisation.

After a short statement, preferably from one speaker, questions may be invited from the journalists. There is no need for this to be dragged out indefinitely. Most press conferences should end within forty minutes. If a photographer is present, your assistance in determining the personalities to be photographed will be needed and you should make sure that the names and positions are correct. Radio or television journalists may need a separate room in which to conduct their interviews. Again, as mentioned earlier in this book, don't be afraid to determine the rough lines of questioning in advance. The interviews will be edited for the news bulletins!

Be helpful without being pushy. Newspeople have noses. They know what they are looking for, and no amount of subtle propaganda will divert them. A news conference is an occasion for establishing contact with journalists which can be built upon later. Relationships established in this way can be of mutual benefit.

Occasionally, you may find yourself with an empty room. The first question is — did you check the day before that your event was in the news diary? If you did and nobody shows up, drop your news release into the media offices, make personal contact with the correspondents who cover your particular subject area, offer to fill them in, and leave it at that. Don't be too disappointed. In these days of cut-backs, newspapers have become more selective in covering events. Anyway, it is not necessary to spend a great deal of money organising a press conference. On occasion, press conferences seem to be an excuse for company personnal or members of an organisation to get together.

THE ROLE OF THE PRESS OFFICER

It is preferable if one person in your organisation is assigned the task of press officer. This task involves:

- liaison with the media
- issuing press releases
- monitoring the press and radio on your particular topic. If you feel wronged, issue a correction. Radio and television producers should be made aware of inaccuracies in their treatment of your organisation. Where there has been a serious error of fact, they should be asked to publish a correction
- encouraging the officials of your organisation to use the media to the advantage of your group
- building up contacts with journalists and freelance feature writers, so that you can call them if necessary
- making available your telephone number at home and work.

A good press officer will be a hustler, always looking for opportunities to promote the image and public knowledge of the organisation.

A good press officer must have the confidence of the officials of the organisation, and be privy to the decision-making process in the group. Alternatively, the press officer should be briefed regularly on stories likely to break or which will be of media interest. In large companies, the press officer will have easy access to the chief executive.

If a special event of some significance is about to happen, prepare a news kit. The ordination of a bishop is one such event that the Catholic Press and Information Office would naturally have to deal with frequently.

A news kit would include the following:

1. A biography of the new bishop. Is there anything unusual about his schooling, his relatives or his past assignments which is newsworthy? An explanation of his choice of coat of arms.
2. Information on the forthcoming ceremony. A brief historical note on the cathedral. Who are the principal ecclesiastical dignitaries participating in the ceremony, especially the ordaining prelate? Anything unusual in the ceremony — dignitaries travelling from abroad, participation by relatives,

features in the offertory procession, participation by local vocational groups.

3. Scripts — a text of the homily with a biographical note on the homilist with a text of the new bishop's remarks, if available. If the occasion is a special event like the Synod of Bishops, a press kit would include a historical note of the history of the Synod, the subject matter of past Synods, the principal participants and how they are chosen. Documentation would include biographies of the national delegates and information about accreditation, press briefings and additional documentation available from other sources.

Chapter Three

Appearing on Television

John Peters, a leading businessman, was invited to appear on a TV chat show to present the management's position in an industrial dispute. He declined to give an immediate answer, but took himself off to London for an intensive one-day briefing, designed to prepare him for a television interview. On returning to Dublin, he telephoned the TV producer and said he would not appear. When questioned afterwards about the blatant squandering of money, he said, 'It was worth every penny of it if only to discover that I will never be suitable material for television.' The moral of the story is vital, namely, know your own limitations.

Despite this cautionary tale, an invitation to appear on television is an opportunity and a challenge rather than a problem. Advertisers pay big money for a television slot. Politicians court television journalists in the hope of a little airtime. Charities and trades unions, the authors of books and plays, all jostle for television time. There are also people who need the exposure that only television can give, to massage their egos.

Free access to the sitting rooms and kitchens of millions of homes is an opportunity not to be passed over lightly. In a television interview you may not get an 'easy ride', but it could be the nearest you will get to eyeball-to-eyeball contact with people you would never otherwise reach.

Radio is a voice to which the listener adds the image. Television depends to a considerable extent, sometimes exclusively, on the visual to make an impact. How often do you recall what a television personality or a politician or a farmer or a priest actually said on television? Television, by and large, presents images of people and things. The viewer's impression of you will remain long after anything you said has been forgotten.

What television can do for a person was illustrated perfectly by the Irangate congressional hearings. Oliver North went in as the 'bogey man' of a squalid piece of American covert political action. By the time he reached the end of his testimony, thousands of Americans were beseeching him to run for the presidency. He demonstrated his fluency in Reaganspeak. He was able to convince a nation of the rightness of his world view — that the others are Bad and he is Good. The 'end justifies the means' philosophy of life was delivered with a quiet, calm self-righteousness that appealed to the heart of a nation frantically seeking an excuse for the deviousness of its leaders. North invoked God and America. Through his medal-encrusted uniform, his jutting, clean-shaven chin, his willingness to take on the congressmen and senators in hand-to-hand combat, he managed to clothe himself in an irresistible nobility that captivated a nation. What he said will hardly be remembered. That is the threat that television poses — images can and sometimes do deceive!

The danger when it comes to religious broadcasting is to presume that the medium and the message are separable. Slick presentation and professional competence can never replace substance. North was shadow, not substance, as the testimony of Secretary Schultz later demonstrated. One has to question the born again televangelists' hyped-up religious verbosity and show-biz approach to religion. Shadow or substance? In a very real way, when it comes to presenting religion or a religious viewpoint on television, the style in which the message is presented **is** its content. For a great many of the viewers, how the message is expressed communicates more than what is expressed, so if there is a disparity between the medium and the message, the medium may prevail. Perhaps the Fr Trendy type of image obscures the solid content of the message. The language, tone and style need to be appropriate to the message and, of course, to the recipient of the message.

Television deals in commodities. News, current affairs, light entertainment, drama, film, documentary, history; almost anything likely to interest large numbers of people is the stuff of television. The electronic media is often hungry for the raw material in which it deals. Occasionally, there isn't enough programming to fill the schedule. Television is not only for the 'stars'. There may be a place for your story or event. It is better to consider television as a potential ally, rather than as an enemy to be kept at arm's length.

The influence of television is considerable. We spend eight years of our lives watching it. At the same time, it is important not to over-emphasise its significance in forming attitudes and opinions. For instance, a market survey taken in June 1983 reported that while Irish people were willing to look to television, and to a lesser extent radio and the press, as primary sources of information about politics and current affairs, this deference to the media was less in evidence in the case of personal or sexual morality. This was not because these areas were considered private, but rather because they fell within a different public domain, one which looked to the Catholic Church as a source of guidance and authority. (See *Television and Irish Society — 21 years of Irish television* — a TRE-IFI publication).

The extent of the influence of television on people is hotly debated. Clive James claims that 'nobody can be sure about what television does to the viewer. One opinion holds that television programmes can subjugate whole populations and turn children into murderers. Another opinion holds that television is too trivial a cultural event to be considered. A surprising number of experts have subscribed to both these opinions in close succession or even simultaneously. (*The Crystal Bucket*, Clive James, Jonathan Cape, 1981, p. 19).

Here is a story about frogs I recall reading some years ago. If you place a frog in a pan of cold water which you gradually heat to boiling point, he will die. On the other hand, pop a frog into a pan of boiling water and he will immediately spring out unharmed. I have a hunch that the influence of television is corrosive and saturation viewing is like sitting in water which is gradually being heated!

Television is a potential ally, but it will never be an adequate substitute for personal contact or for a sermon well prepared and delivered with style and conviction. No doubt, people will pose the question — If Jesus were alive today would he use television? I think the answer is yes — and no. The primary thrust of Jesus' ministry was to the few. John, the three special friends, the rest of the apostles, the seventy-two, and only then, the crowds. Television is brash and breathless, always demanding the newest, the biggest, the brightest. I can hardly imagine television being anything other than an important secondary aid in helping people into a personal relationship with Jesus Christ. All of the media can be claimed for Christ, but probably only as a preparation.

SO YOU WANT YOUR STORY COVERED?

Count yourself very lucky when the local television station rings you seeking an interview or inviting you to participate in a chat show.

Television does not have the capacity to react as immediately as other media. Therefore, advance warning is vital. As with newspapers, television news and current affairs departments have regular editorial meetings. With television, the location of camera crews and their availability will often be a determining factor. You will be competing with stories that have a national dimension.

When Paul Harrison of the film production company Worldvoice, returned from filming the Ethiopian famine in July 1984, he carried with him the most remarkable footage. He contacted the BBC. They were vaguely interested, but said they would be sending a crew into Ethiopia in a day or two. In fact, it took three months before the famous Michael Buerk film broke the horror of the famine to the world. The ITV network was offered the film. Their comment was, 'Sorry. Africa isn't really an easy story to tell. The public feel it's too far from them and a famine isn't really a nice news item. (Paul Harrison and Robin Palmer, *News out of Africa*, Hilary Shipman, 1986).' So, what became a universal story, culminating with Bob Geldof and Live

Aid, was let slip by the major British TV networks. It didn't rate as news worthy of national coverage at that time.

The average news item on TV lasts only 2-3 minutes. A story that can consume acres of newsprint jostles for a comment and a picture on TV. In order to receive national news coverage on TV your story needs to have some unusual angle to it! Nevertheless, it is always worth sending the press release of your event or story (see p. 95).

Many TV networks carry a magazine-type programme as an addendum to the national evening news. Try to reach the producer of the programme. In general, you can find out the name of the producer by ringing the switchboard of the TV station. If you can offer good transparencies to accompany an interview or to be used with a 'voice-over' as a news item, you will stand a better chance of getting on the airwaves.

Like the print media, TV networks have specialist departments — sport, religion, current affairs, books, children, agriculture. If your story fits into an existing category ask to speak to the special correspondent. It is often the people with the most contacts and 'know how' who manage to make it to the airwaves.

Many large companies, political parties and Churches have their own press and information office. These offices are staffed by media professionals who have developed contacts and who are available as spokespersons for their special interest group. For instance, the Catholic Press and Information Office at Booterstown Avenue, Co. Dublin, acts on behalf of the Irish Hierarchy of the Roman Catholic Church.

WHAT'S NEWS?

What is news for TV? When are you news? The usual criteria for what constitutes news include: immediacy, proximity, consequence, conflict, prominence, suspense, special features.

1. Is it interesting or important to a large number of people? The school play is probably of the utmost interest to parents and participants, but to others it is a non-event.
2. Is it controversial? An item like a planning application that involves the demolition of a local artisan housing complex

might be such an example. A life support machine being turned off with consequent death to the patient is another.

3. Is it a 'first'? The Guinness Book of Records syndrome will tend to attract the TV.
4. Are any famous people involved — film stars, politicians, visiting dignitaries?
5. Is adventure involved — a mountain climbing expedition or an Atlantic crossing in a bath tub or in a balloon?
6. Is it novel? The weird, different, unusual and a creative angle will help sell your story.
7. Does it have consequences that will change the future? The closing of a local primary school would be such an example.

Let us take an imaginary case. St David's is a new special school for retarded children. It is about to open a miniature shopping centre on the school complex to assist the young people in their future integration into society. The new unit will be opened by the Minister for Youth Affairs.

Answer the questions: What? Where? Who? When? How? Why?

In answering these questions for yourself, be sensitive to the special features that this new initiative encompasses, the benefits it will confer on clients and what makes it truly unique.

YOU'RE ON NEXT

You have been invited to appear on a current affairs programme! The researcher or PA has rung you up with a note of urgency in his voice. His job is to seek an immediate commitment from you to appear on the show. He may even have asked a number of potential participants without success. You do not have to give an immediate answer. If you want time to think or to consult someone, say so and promise to ring back.

In general, 'if they come to you, you're in the driving seat', could be a handy rule of thumb. Get some basic information about the show you have been asked to appear on.

Find out the nature of the programme and assess the level of comment and information expected of you. How many unsuspecting interviewees jump in at the deep end and remain floundering thereafter?

It is quite normal, indeed it will be expected of you, to ask some of the following questions:

a) What is the show and who is the presenter or interviewer?
b) Is the show live or recorded?
c) If recorded, will it be edited?
d) Who else will be appearing on the show?
e) What is the format and what type of questions are you likely to be asked?
f) Where will it be held and when?
g) Who is the audience and will they be invited to participate?

Don't be too inquisitorial or belligerent. You may miss a golden opportunity.

The researcher on a regular news show is at the bottom of the television journalists' pyramid. As the name implies, he does the research. Virtually all the work in setting up an interview comes under the heading of research, so on a straightforward interview you may never meet the producer at all. A serious current affairs show will employ serious investigative journalists. Their research into a story may take weeks. They will look for supporting documentation or collaborative evidence. An example of this type of show would be the famous **Today Tonight** current affairs programme on moneylending which resulted in a public enquiry when it was screened by RTE.

News reporters 'on the beat' will have considerable control over the stories they report. The nature of the questions asked will be at their discretion, as will the linking commentary. Invariably, a researcher will not be able to give you firm guarantees about how the story will be handled.

THE ARGUMENTS FOR AND AGAINST APPEARING ON TELEVISION
For
a) Failure to comment may leave the programme without anyone representing your point of view. The result could be a statement like 'Church authorities, when invited to

appear on the programme, declined the invitation'. This can plant a suspicion in the viewer's mind that you had something to hide.

b) If you are co-operative on this occasion, further opportunities for appearing on television may present themselves.

c) This interview may provide the opportunity to clarify, explain or present a point of view that has been misunderstood.

d) You will reach millions of people at no cost to yourself.

Against

a) You are inexperienced and aware of the possibility that you may fall flat on your face. However, don't forget that a normal anxiety sets the adrenalin flowing.

b) You are unwilling to take the risk of injuring your case.

c) You don't want to be questioned on the particular subject because a skilled interviewer may extract information from you that could be detrimental to your case.

d) You don't know enough about the subject and aren't in a position to be briefed sufficiently.

e) You are afraid that your superiors will disagree with your point of view and, therefore, you risk retribution!

f) You will have insufficient time to do justice to the subject.

On balance, lean in favour of accepting the invitation.

HARD WORK — IMAGINATION — FAITH

Through sheer hard work, much of it boring and repetitive, media people have honed their profession to a fine art. Talent and flair are also necessary ingredients for success. For one who is called upon infrequently to appear on television hard work is also essential. Research and preparation may be the key to a successful interview.

Imagination has been defined as creative ability. I suppose it is the opposite of dull, boring, routine. To think in images and to present a point of view from a new perspective is not always easy and yet that is what will interest the listener and viewer.

When a Churchperson is asked to appear on television or speak on the radio he or she is not asked as a politician but as a person who is commited to a particular way of life and subscribes to a particular set of beliefs. This is important. The viewers don't want to see or hear more politics, this time from a man in a dog-collar! What is the faith dimension of what you have to say? Invariably, Church personnel will talk about anything except their faith. They don't want to be thought of as pious or sentimental. How often have you heard a Church spokesperson mention the name of Jesus? How often have you heard a witness or testimony to faith from a Church spokesperson? I am not saying that Jesus or testimonies of faith have to be part of every media interview but at the very least they ought not to be deliberatey excluded.

Keep the visual aspect of the medium in mind. Philosophical waffle is difficult for the viewer to comprehend. Make what you have to say specific. When I say **animal** — what comes into your mind? A vague collage of different animals perhaps! If I say **dog** — what happens? You think of a particular dog. Be specific! If you say 'There are one thousand people without shoes in Townley village — the response could well be — so what! If on the other hand you can say — 'Today in the fourth class in Townley National School one in three of the children has no shoes to walk to school in', the receiver gets a picture. One thousand, as against one in three in fourth class, makes all the difference when you are communicating your message.

PREPARATION

Preparation is vital! The best place to start is to think about the nature of the interview you are going to do. It is going to be a conversation about two special characteristics: it is going to be steered and it is going to be short. The steering will nominally be in the hands of the interviewer.

1. Brief yourself thoroughly on the subject. Isolate **two or three** of the essential points that you want to get across to the viewer. Write them down to help you memorise them but not for actual use on the programme. Television and radio are surprisingly bad at conveying detailed information. So don't try to read out the Annual Report or give a complete

account of your religion from the Fall to the Second Coming.

2. Either ask someone to do devil's advocate in a mock 'role play' situation or anticipate the questions you are likely to be asked.

3. Have a general overview of the possible answers you will give, **avoiding trade jargon**.

4. If there are to be other participants on the programme, anticipate the points on which you may be asked to comment.

5. If necessary, don't be afraid to memorise **a snatch** of what you wish to say.

6. Do you have an anecdote or personal story to illustrate your point? If you do, make sure it is **brief**.

Media personnel often come across as being either egoistic or belligerent. Despite the public image, like people in other walks of life, they are considerate and helpful off-screen. Identify with the reporter, editor/producer — appreciate the position of newspeople who are under severe constraints of time and space to produce and develop a story. They work long hours under considerable stress.

Strike a balance between agreeing to everything and adopting a hostile and unfriendly attitude.

IMMEDIATE PREPARATION

1. Arrive on time. You will be requested to attend well in advance of the scheduled time. This may be irritating, on the other hand it gives the opportunity for an informal chat with any other participants. You will collect information which will be useful to you in the forthcoming interview. If the show is to be taped for future screening, you may have an opportunity to discuss the topic with the presenter in advance.

2. Dress is important. Television is about images, so be presentable. Medium or dark colours show you off to the best advantage. Avoid badges, chains, noisy jewellery.

3. Do use make up. In general, if well applied, it flatters!

4. Nerves — everyone gets nervous about appearing on

television or before a lot of people. It is nature's way of bringing you to your peak performance. Don't be afraid to mention it to the interviewer, who probably feels nervous also.

THE TELEVISION STUDIO

First impressions of a televsion studio can be intimidating. Bright arc lights will hang from an overhead gantry. Monitor screens will be placed at strategic points in the studio. Cameras and cables will make the available space appear cluttered. Perhaps a boom microphone mounted on a 'dolly' will be ready for action, particularly when a studio audience is participating. The crew, consisting of a floor manager, sound engineers, camera operators, PAs and others, will take very little notice of you — they have seen it all before, many times. A 'voice level' will be taken, usually by the interviewer asking you some trivial question. A clapperboard, like the studio clock, is a visual label for a shot. It is placed in front of the camera to give an easy point of synchronisation in the cutting room.

Don't allow the sophisticated gadgetry to mesmerise you. It is better to ignore the monitor screens, particularly when the interview is in progress. The operating camera being used will have a red light on, an indication that the camera is 'live'.

THE INTERVIEW

1. Obey the instructions you receive from the studio personnel. They are trained and paid to ensure that you are presented to the best advantage. Therefore, don't interfere with the microphones, props, setting, etc.
2. Seat yourself comfortably, but don't slouch. If you are too 'laid back', it gives a couldn't-care-less impression.
3. In a television interview you are 'speaking' to one person, the interviewer. Consider the wider viewing public as important eavesdroppers. You don't have to shout, preach, lecture or harangue. Bellicosity is unlikely to help your case. Speak naturally as you would to an interested acquaintance.
4. Don't be afraid to use your hands if that is your usual style.
5. Establish yourself with authority and conviction in the first

113

twenty seconds. If you are asked a totally unexpected question, then you may reasonably use the technique of saying 'I will come back to that in a moment, but the important issue here is ....'

6. Don't be afraid to challenge the interviewer. You should never let the interviewer away with a statement that is untrue or tendentious.

7. **Keep it short.** Don't get involved in long convoluted stories — you encourage the risk of being cut off in mid-sentence. The viewers will run out on patience unless you present your position concisely, clearly and briefly.

8. Don't fill embarrassing silences — that is the interviewer's job: the silence may be contrived in the hope that more information may be elicited from you.

9. Don't interrupt yourself with 'um', 'ah', 'well', 'eh', 'like', 'you know' and so on. This can happen unconsciously — that is why preparation is important. Most people who are hesitant and fumbling are unaware of it until the video reveals the whole truth.

10. You can take the initiative without waiting for another question. If you get your points across in a cogent and interesting fashion you may not be interrupted.

11. Above all be simple. What percentage of the viewers know the meaning of terms like: ministry, liturgy, ambo, conciliar, lectern, synod, inculturation, lay minister, catechetics, plain chant, Old Testament, annulment, sacramental, reconciliation? **Don't use clichés, clerical jargon or churchy language — it will be a big turn-off.**

For example, the editor of the *London Times* was explaining on television the highly complex theory of the relationship of money supply to inflation over a period of time. He said, 'The money supply is like a tap attached to a hosepipe which is two years long. Once the tap has been turned on at one end, nothing can stop it coming out at the other end.' Try to illustrate your point.

12. Don't 'mix it' with other participants in an argumentative way. Do politicians have a bad name partly because they revel in shouting one another down in any media

discussion? If you have to interrupt or correct, do so with courtesy.

13. **The panel interview is the most difficult to handle**. Panels are about seizing the available opportunities with both hands. When you get an opportunity to speak, keep speaking — you will be interrupted. Try to catch the chairperson's eye — when you do, speak.

14. Don't allow yourself to be put in the dock! Present your case in a positive fashion. Be on your guard for the common techniques used by interviewers to distance themselves from the criticism. For instance, 'How do you answer the criticism many people are making today about unfeeling authoritarianism of Church leaders?' asks the interviewer. Or, 'Isn't the lack of consultation in the appointment of bishops against everything the Council stood for?'

15. Don't lean over and start having an animated conversation the moment the interviewer has ended. Your microphone might still be live. Just sit and wait until the interviewer moves.

16. Humour is not out of place if it is natural to you. Therefore, don't be afraid to smile. However, jokes like 'Did you hear the one about....?' variety will invite immediate interruption, except in a long personal John Freedman type interview.

THE INTERVIEWER

Sir Robin Day has long been acknowledged as the doyen of Britain's television interviewers. In his book, *Television: A Personal Report* (1961), he writes:

> I can never understand why more people, especially eminent ones, do not hit back at incompetent interviewers, or even competent ones. If he has not done his homework or clarified his thoughts the interviewer deserves to be slapped down.

He suggests a code for television interviewers that might be helpful to potential interviewees.

1. The television interviewer must do his duty as a journalist, probing for facts and opinions.
2. He should set his own prejudices aside and put questions which reflect various opinions, disregarding probable accusations of bias.
3. He should not allow himself to be overawed in the presence of a powerful person.
4. He should not compromise the honesty of the interview by omitting awkward topics or by rigging questions in advance.
5. He should resist any inclination in those employing him to soften or rig an interview so as to secure a 'prestige' appearance, or to please.
6. He should not submit his questions in advance, but it is reasonable to state the main areas of questioning. If he submits specific questions before, he is powerless to put any supplementary questions, which may be vitally needed to clarify or challenge an answer.
7. He should give fair opportunity to answer questions, subject to the time limits imposed by television.
8. He should never take advantage of his professional experience to trap or embarrass someone unused to television appearances.
9. He should press his questions firmly and persistently, but not tediously, offensively, or merely in order to sound tough.
10. He should remember that a television interviewer is not employed as a debater, prosecutor, inquisitor, psychiatrist or third degree expert, but as a journalist seeking information on behalf of the viewer.

Appendix 1

Standards in Broadcasting and Complaints Procedure in Ireland and Great Britain

The Broadcasting Authority (Amendment) Act 1987 — Ireland

Conditions which apply to Broadcasting in Ireland

The Act states that 'the Authority shall in its programming be responsible to the interests and concern of the whole community, be mindful of the need for understanding and peace with the whole island of Ireland, ensure that the programmes reflect the varied elements which make up the culture of the people of the whole island of Ireland, and have special regard for elements which distinguish that culture and in particular for the Irish language'.

In addition to objectivity and impartiality, the Act states:

News

All news broadcasts by the authority must be reported and presented in an objective and impartial manner and without any expression of the Authority's own views.

Current affairs

The broadcast treatment of current affairs, including matters which are either of public controversy or the subject of current public debate, must be fair to all interests concerned and without any expression of the Authority's own views.

Privacy

Another requirement is that 'the Authority shall not, in its programmes and in the means employed to make sure programmes, unreasonably encroach on the privacy of an individual'.

COMPLAINING ABOUT PROGRAMMES

Broadcasting Complaints Commission

The Commission replaces the earlier broadcasting Complaints Advisory Committee. The ambit of the Commission competence is confined to three areas:

News

Complaints that in broadcasting a specified item of news the Authority did not report and present it in an object and impartial manner and without any expression of the Authority's own views, or failed to comply with the prohibition to broadcast anything which might reasonably be regarded as being likely to promote or incite to crime or as tending to undermine the Authority.

Current affairs

Complaints that the Authority failed to be fair to all interests concerned or to present the broadcast matter in an objective and impartial manner, and without any expression of the Authority's own views ...

Privacy

Complaints that on a specified occasion the Authority in a programme, or in the means employed to make such programme, unreasonably encroached on the privacy of an individual.

Complaints shoule be addressed to:
    The Secretary
    Broadcasting Complaints Commission
    P.O. Box 913
    Dublin 2.

Conditions which apply to broadcasting in Britain

The Television Act 1954 and the Broadcasting Act 1981 oblige the Independent Broadcasting Authority, so far as possible, not to transmit anything which 'offends against good taste or decency or is likely to encourage or incite to crime or lead to disorder or to be offensive to public feeling' and 'that the programmes maintain aproper balance ...'

The Chairman of the BBC accepted on behalf of the Corporation these same conditions as recently as April 1981. (See Licence and Agreement, Cmnd 8233, HMSO). The BBC is set up by Royal Charter. The Broadcasting Authorities also issue, from time to time, guidance notes to producers on programme content, notably violence, and editorial policy. These can be obtained from BBC Publications.

Complaining about programmes

Several courses of action are open to members of the public:

a) **The Broadcasting Complaints Commission**, 20 Albert Embankment, London SE1 7TL.
NB: This Commission does **not** consider complaints about programme content. It deals only with complaints about misrepresentation and/or invasion of privacy.

b) **The duty officer:** The BBC have a duty officer on duty most of the time. The independent companies do not have a duty officer as such, but someone will always take a message. They are there only to record comments so that they may be passed on to the right person or department. The duty officer is not the BBC or the IBA and is not responsible for the programmes, so one should not direct angry feelings towards this person, but should simply say that you feel angry/upset/offended etc.

Always try to follow up a telephone call with a letter to the Director General of the BBC, IBA or RTE.

c) **Writing that letter:** Always mention the name of the programme, the date, the time and the channel on which it was transmitted. Describe precisely what you are complaining about and explain why you think your complaint is valid. Always be

119

reasonable and courteous. Offer suggestions on how the programme could have been improved so that these ideas can be considered for the next programme. You will never persuade or convince anyone with angry rhetoric.

d) Who to write to: Who you write to depends on the seriousness of the complaint or, of course, the degree of praise.

Write to the producer of the programme. Try to find out his/her name from the *RTE Guide*, *Radio Times* or *TV Times*. Address personally, rather than Dear Sir/Madan. Write to the Director General. Write to the Chairman. Write to your TD or MP. If replies from the Broadcasting Authorities are not satisfactory take the matter up with your TD or MP. Send copies of the correspondence and say why you feel the reply is not satisfactory. Alternatively, if the matter is serious, write directly to your TD or MP asking him/her to take up the complaint with the RTE or BBC/IBA. Parliament is ultimately responsible for broadcasting. In Britain the Home Office is the Government Department with overall responsibility.

Right to Reply — TV programme on Channel 4: This provides a unique means of complaining or praising via their **Video Box**. These are situated at Channel 4 TV, Charlotte Street, London and also at Glasgow. Gus Macdonald, the presenter of the programme says 'We must train people to protest ... write, phone. It is your right — your reply to reply.' The **Video Box** is like a photo booth. You simply go in, sit down and make your comment straight to camera. It is a good idea to write out what you want to say in advance.

Monitoring programmes
If aggrieved by the treatment of a cause in programmes try to organise a monitoring project of all current affairs programmes for, say, six months. Evidence of bias is essential in order to be able to substantiate claims.

General points to consider
a) Many people feel aggrieved by some media coverage or issues in which they are involved.

b) It should not be assumed that producers are hostile to your cause. They may simply lack information or knowledge.

c) Try to make news. Always be on the offensive. Don't wait for opposing views to be reported and then fight a rearguard action. Local organisations should take the initiative by issuing news stories, thus making the running. Contact local radio stations. Let them know what you are doing, whether it be public meetings, counselling, picketing, fun runs or whatever.

d) Be on the lookout for opportunities to write. For example, listen to the **Today** programme BBC Radio 4; **The World at One, The World this Weekend, Any Questions?** These programmes have letters spots. Also the **Radio Times** and **TV Times** have letters pages. So do the national daily newspapers.

e) Radio phone-ins — ring up and say you would like to talk about, for example 'this report by so and so published today/the other day. I think such and such'.

Appendix 2

Standards in Journalism and Complaints Procedures

It is difficult to operate as a journalist without being a member of the National Union of Journalists. On obtaining membership of the Union the new member is given a document entitled *Code of Professional Conduct*. This is the 'operator's manual' for the working journalist. The code is strict and if adhered to would raise the standard of journalism appreciably. However, it is seldom referred to and in my experience most journalists of any expeience are either unaware of the existence of the code or unaware of its contents. A cursory glance at any tabloid newspaper will bear this out. Unions are justly vigiliant of their members' rights. In the profession of journalism there appears to be less regard, particularly in recent years, to the journalist's duties. That is why it is important that the general public be aware that a code exists which can be appealed to in case of dispute.

NUJ Code of Professional Conduct
1. A journalist has a duty to maintain the highest professional and ethical standards.
2. A journalist shall at all times defend the principle of the freedom of the Press and other media in relation to the collection of information and the expression of comment and criticism. He/she shall strive to eliminate distortion, news suppression and censorship.
3. A journlist shall strive to ensure that the information he/she

disseminates is fair and accurate, avoid the expression of comment and conjecture as establihed fact and falsification by distortion, selection or misrepresentation.

4. A journalist shall rectify promptly any harmful inaccuracies, ensure that correction and aplogies receive due prominence and afford the right to reply to persons critised when the issue is of sufficient importance.

5. A journalist shall obtain information, photographs and illustrations only by straightforward means. The use of other means can be justified only by over-riding considerations of the public interest. The journalist is entitled to exercise a personal conscientious objection to the use of such means.

6. Subject to justification by over-riding considerations of the public interest, a journalist shall do nothing which entails intrusion into private grief and distress.

7. A journalist shall protect confidential sources of information.

8. A journalist shall not accept bribes not shall he/she allow other inducements to influence the performance of his/her professional duties.

9. A journalist shall not lend himself/herself to the distortion or suppression of the truth because of advertising or other considerations.

10. A journalist shall only mention a person's age, race, colour, creed, illegitimacy, disability, marital status (or lack of it), gender or sexual orientation if this information is strictly relevant. A journalist shall neither originate or process material which encourages discrimination, ridicule, prejudice or hatred on any of the above grounds.

11. A journalist shall not take private advantage of information gained in the course of his/her duties, before the information is public knowledge.

12. A journalist shall not by way of statement, voice, or appearance endorse by advertisement any commercial product or service save for the promotion of his/her own work or of the medium by which he/she is employed.

A breach of the code of conduct renders a member of the NUJ liable to a complaint being made to the Union's Ethics Council and disciplinary proceedings being undertaken.

How to make a complaint

1. If you have a complaint you may prefer to write direct to the editor of the publication concerned in the first place. The simplest and quickest way of seeking a prompt correction of any inaccuracy is to write direct to the editor.

2. Alternatively, if you wish to complain about material published in a British newspaper or periodical, you may prefer to send full particulars of your complaint (including a copy of any relevant published material) to the director of the Press Council at 1 Salisbury Square, London EC4Y 8AE. He will acknowledge your letter and forward a copy of it to the editor without making any comment about the matter. This gives editors the chance to take any action they think fit including responding directly to you if they wish.

3. Keep copies of all letters you send to the newspaper or periodical and all those you receive from it.

4. If you are not satisfied with the editor's response or if you do not receive any response within a reasonable time — say seven days — and you want to pursue your complaint through the Council write again to the director sending him:

(a) a statement of your complaint saying what you think was improper on the part of the newspaper, periodical or journal and why you think it was wrong;

(b) copies of all letters sent to the editor or those acting for him or her;

(c) all letters from the editor or those acting for him or her;

(d) the page of the newspaper or periodical containing the matter about which you are complaining if the complaint is about something which has been published.

Note: Any document you submit to the Council in presenting your complaint will be retained in the Council's case records and submission of documents is taken as evidence that you accept this rule.

5. In certain cases it is helpful if you forward signed and dated statements by witnesses in support of your complaint. If you do this, please supply the names and addresses of witnesses.

You may decide to do this on your own initiative but the director will tell you if he thinks such statements would be helpful.

6. Where a complaint concerns someone other than the complainants (for example a person referred to in the item complained of) the Council may require the complainant to seek that person's views before the complaint goes forward for adjudication, or the Council itself may seek their views.

Appendix 3

Religious Broadcasting in Ireland and Great Britain

In a free democratic country like Ireland where nearly 80% of the people practise their religion, one would expect high quality religious programming. In fact, the opposite is true. At the time of writing the national broadcasting organisation, Radio Telefis Éireann, doesn't even have a Department of Religious Broadcasting! It was dismantled a number of years ago.

In our neighbouring island, Britain, where the level of religious practice in the established Church of England is less than 10%, the quality and time given to religious programmes is excellent. David Winter, Head of Religious Broadcasting in the BBC, claims that their programmes for adults 'do set out to reinforce faith'. No such claim has ever been made for what passes for religious programming on RTE.

In RTE religious programmes fall neatly into two categories: liturgical and devotional onthe one hand and discussion type programmes on the other. When religious matters are dealt with in other programme areas, they are often treated in a superficial manner, rather in the vein of an adolescent iconoclasm whose aim is to shock, or to be controversial for the sake of controversy. The extraordinary news treatment of a successor to the Roman Catholic See of Dublin is a case in point.

Perhaps the point I am trying to make can best be illustrated by examining how the broadcasting magazines, the *RTE Guide* in Ireland and the *Radio Times* in Britain, dealt with Holy Week, the high point of the Christian's year. Then a glance at the religious schedules of the BBC's Radio 4, compared with those of RTE's Radio 1, will adequately demonstrate the commitment to religious broadcasting in so-called 'pagan Britain' and the extraordinary failure of Irish broadcasting to do more than 'doff its cap' in the direction of religion. Incidentally, lack of resources can hardly be the reason for Ireland's failure, as the state broadcasting organisation, RTE, made a substantial profit in 1987 and expects to continue to do so.

Radio Times

Cover for Holy Week: A full colour reproduction of an alterpiece by Raphael, 'The Crucified Christ with the Virgin Mary, Saints and Angels'.

Editorial content on programmes: Two full pages with two photographs in colour and one in black and white were devoted to holy Week programmes on radio and TV.
This item comes first in the table of contents.
In the daily schedule Friday is referred to as 'Good Friday'.

RTE Guide

Cover for Holy Week: Photograph of a pop star!

Editorial content on programmes: One half-page, with black and white photograph devoted to Holy Week programmes on radio and TV. An additional half-page, with colour reproduction, deals with a Good Friday programme on radio. Only the first of these items is listed in the table of contents, at thirteenth place in a list of twenty-seven.
In the daily schedule Friday is simply listed as 'Friday'.

Time specially devoted to Holy Week Themes

BBC 3:	8 hrs 40 mins.	RTE 1:	8 hrs 19 mins.
BBC 4:	6 hrs 13 mins.	Irish language:	30 mins.
Total:	*14 hrs 53 mins.*		*8 hrs 49 mins.*

Weekly Schedule of Religious Programmes
BBC 4   *RTE Radio 1*

Monday-Friday	*Monday-Friday*
6.25 a.m. Prayer for the Day a reflection	7.25 a.m. Just a Thought*
	10.57 a.m. Repeat of above
7.45 a.m. Thought for the Day — A comment on a contemporary issue	*Monday*
10.45 a.m. Daily Service A live act of worship	10.10 p.m. Addendum — report on current affairs and ideas
Saturdays	*Saturdays*
6.50 a.m. Prayer for the Day	7.27 a.m. Smaoineamh
7.45 a.m. In perspective A note by the BBC Religious Affairs Correspondent	11.52 a.m. Repeat of above
10.15 p.m. Evening Service — A late-night preparation for Sunday	
Sundays	*Sundays*
6.30 a.m. Morning Has Broken — Music for Sunday Morning	
7.50 a.m. Turning Over New Leaves. A religious book review	
8.15 a.m. A weekly 'live' news magazine on religious matters	
9.30 a.m. Morning Service direct from a Church	9.30 a.m. Mass
	10.20 a.m. Religious Service
11.00 p.m. Seeds of Faith	9.30 p.m. Dialogue* — Conversation with guests.

*Note: All the above details given here are as officially provided by both RTE and BBC. However, in the case of RTE, the inclusion of **Just a Thought** and **Dialogue** as regular religious programmes is questionable. They may aim to evoke nice feelings and concern, but that does not necessarily make them religious in content or purpose.

Bibliography

ACTON, Kenneth, *Starting in Video*, Jay Books, 1986

BAISTOW, Tom, *Fourth Rate Estate*, Comedia Publishing Group, 1985
BLAND, Michael, *You're on Next!*, Kogan Page, 1979
BROOKS, Peter, *Communicating Conviction*, Epworth Press, 1983

CONRAD, Peter, *Television — the medium and its manners*, Routledge & Kegan Paul, 1982
COONEY, John, *No News is Bad News*, Veritas Publications, 1974

DEL MUNDO, Eduardo (ed), *Philippine Mass Media*, Communications Foundation for Asia, 1986
DUNKLEY, Christopher, *Television Today and Tomorrow — Wall-to-Wall Dallas?* Penguin Books, 1985
DUNN, Joseph, *No Tigers in Africa*, The Columba Press, 1986

ELVY, Peter, *Buying Time*, McCrimmon Publishing Co. Ltd, 1986
EMSWILER, Tom Neufer, *Making the Most of Video in Religious Settings*, Jay Books, 1986
EVANS, Harold, *Editing and Design*, Heinemann, 1972

GLASGOW UNIVERSITY MEDIA GROUP, *Bad News*, Routledge & Kegan Paul, 1978
GOODHART, David and WINTOUR, Patrick, *Eddie Shah and the Newspaper Revolution*, Coronet Books, 1986
GREENFIELD, Patricia Marks, *Mind and Media — the effects of television, video games and computers*, Harvard University Press, 1984

HADDEN, Jeffrey and SWANN, Charles, *Prime Time Preachers*, Addison-Wesley, 1981
HARRISON, Paul and PALMER, Robin, *News Out of Africa*, Hilary Shipman, 1986
HARTLEY, John, *Understanding News*, Methuen, 1982
HEALY, Tim, *Strange But True*, Octopus, 1984
HORSFIELD, Peter, *Religious Television — the American Experience*, Longman, 1984

Inter Mirifica, [Decree on the Means of Social Communications], CTS, London, 1967

Irish Values and Attitudes, [Report of the European Value System Study], Dominican Publications, 1984

LONG, Mark, *A Guide to Satellite TV*, Radio Shack, 1985

LYON, David, *The Silicon Society — How will information technology change our lives?*, Lion Publishing, 1986

MANN, Peter, *Through Words and Images*, CTNA, 1985

Many Voices, One World, [Report by the International Commission for the Study of Communication Problems] (McBride), Kogan Page, 1981

McLOONE, Martin and McMAHON, John (eds), *Television and Irish Society*, RTE and Irish Film Institute, 1984

McLUHAN, Eric, *Understanding Media*, Ark Paperbacks, 1964

McQUAIL, Denis (ed), *Sociology of Mass Communications*, Penguin, 1972

McSHANE, Denis, *Using the Media*, Pluto Press, 1979

MORRIS, Colin, *God in the Box*, Hodder & Stoughton, 1984

NAISBITT, John, *Megatrends*, Warner Books, 1981

PRONE, Terry, *Write and get paid for it!*, Turoe Press, 1979

QUAIL, Denis and SIUNE, Karen (eds), *New Media Politics — Comparative Perspectives in Western Europe*, Sage Publications, 1986

See for Yourself: A Guide to the Use of Video by the Christian Community, Jay Books, 1985

THOMPSON, Denys (ed), *Discrimination and Popular Culture*, Penguin Books, 1964

THORN, William J. (ed) *A Vision All Can Share*, US Catholic Conference, 1984

TRABER, Michael (ed), *The Myth of the Information Revolution*, Sage Publications, 1986

VATICAN II, *Communio et Progressio* [Pastoral Instruction on the Means of Social Communication] Dominican Publications, 1971

WHITAKER, Brian, *News Ltd*, Minority Press Group, 1981

WILDMON, Donald E., *The Home Invaders*, Victor Books, 1985

WILLIAMS, Raymond, *Communications*, Penguin Books, 1962